The Consecrated Way

TO CHRISTIAN PERFECTION
by *Alonzo T. Jones*

THE UPWARD WAY

P.O. Box 717 Dodge Center
Minnesota, 55927
Printed in the U.S.A.
by Pacific Press Publishing Association
Boise, Idaho

Adventist Classics Series

4157

©1988 by *The Upward Way*
printed 1988 — 25,000 copies
The Upward Way
Dodge Center, Minnesota 55927

ISBN-0-945-460-02-3
COVER DESIGN: ED GUTHERO
PHOTO: GENE SASSE

Table of Contents

Introduction

In the manifestation of Christ the Saviour it is revealed that He must appear in the three offices of prophet, priest, and king.

Of Him as prophet it was written in the days of Moses: "I will raise them up a Prophet from among their brethren, like unto thee, and will put My words in His mouth; and He shall speak unto them all that I shall command Him. And it shall come to pass, that whosoever will not hearken unto My words which He shall speak in My name, I will require it of him." Deut. 18:18, 19. And this thought was continued in the succeeding scriptures until His coming.

Of Him as priest it was written in the days of David: "The Lord hath sworn, and will not repent, Thou art a priest forever after the order of Melchizedek." Ps. 110:4. This thought was also continued in the Scriptures, not only until His coming, but after His coming.

And of Him as king it was written in the days of David: "Yet have I set ["anointed," margin] My King upon My holy hill of Zion." Ps. 2:6. And this thought, likewise, was continued in all the scriptures afterward unto His coming, after His coming, and unto the end of the Book.

Thus the Scriptures abundantly present Him in the three offices of prophet, priest, and king.

This threefold truth is generally recognized by all who have acquaintance with the Scriptures; but above this there is the truth which seems to be *not* so well known—that He is *not all three of these at the same time*. The three offices are successive. He is prophet first, then after that He is priest, and after that He is king.

He was "that Prophet" when He came into the world, as that "Teacher come from God," the Word made flesh and dwelling among us, "full of grace and truth." Acts 3:19–23. But He was not then a priest, nor would He be a priest if He were even yet on earth; for it is written, "If He were on earth, He should not be a priest." Heb. 8:4. But, having finished His work in His prophetic office on earth, and having ascended to heaven at the right hand of the throne of God, He is now and there our "great High Priest," who "ever liveth to make intercession for us," as it is written: "He shall be a priest upon His [Father's] throne: and the counsel of peace shall be between them both." Zech. 6:12, 13.

As He was not *that Priest* when He was on earth as *that Prophet;* so *now* He is not *that King* when He is in heaven as *that Priest.* True, He is king in the sense and in the fact that He is upon His Father's throne; and thus He is the kingly priest and the priestly king after the order of Melchizedek, who, though priest of the Most High God, was also King of Salem, which is King of peace. Heb. 7:1, 2. But this is not the kingly office and throne that is referred to, and that is contemplated in the prophecy and the promise of His specific office as king.

The kingly office of the promise and the prophecy is that He shall be King upon "the throne of His father David," in perpetuation of the kingdom of God upon this earth. This kingly office is the restoration and the perpetuation, in Him, of the diadem, the crown, and the throne of David, which was discontinued when, because of the profanity and wickedness of the king and people of Judah and Israel, they were taken captive to Babylon, when it was declared: "And thou, profane wicked prince of Israel, whose day is come, when iniquity shall have an end, Thus saith the Lord God; Remove the diadem, and take off the crown: this shall not be the same: exalt him that is low, and abase him that is high. I will overturn, overturn, overturn, it: and it shall be no more, until He come whose right it is; and I will give it Him." Eze. 21:25–27.

Thus and at that time the throne, the diadem, and the crown of the kingdom of David was discontinued "until He come whose right it is," when it will be given Him. And He whose right it is, is only Christ, "the son of David." And this "coming" was not His first coming when He came in His humiliation, a man of sorrows and acquainted with grief; but it is His second coming, when He comes in His glory as "King of kings and Lord of lords," when His kingdom shall break in pieces and consume all the kingdoms of earth, and shall occupy the whole earth, and shall stand forever.

It is true that when He was born into the world, a babe in

Bethlehem, He was born King, and was then and has been ever since King by right. But it is equally true that this kingly office, diadem, crown, and throne of the prophecy and promise, He did not then take, and has not yet taken, and will not take *until He comes again. Then* it will be that He will take to Himself His great power upon this earth, and will reign fully and truly in all the splendor of His kingly office and glory. For in the Scripture it is portrayed that *after* "the judgment was set, and the books were opened," one like the Son of man came to the Ancient of days, "and there was given Him dominion, and glory, and a kingdom, that all people, nations, and languages, should serve Him: His dominion is an everlasting dominion, which shall not pass away, and His kingdom that which shall not be destroyed." Dan. 7:13, 14. *Then it is* that He shall indeed take "the throne of His father David: and He shall reign over the house of Jacob forever; and of His kingdom there shall be no end." Luke 1:32, 33.

Thus it is plain that in the contemplation of the scripture, in the contemplation of the promise and the prophecy, as to His three offices of prophet, priest, and king, these offices are successive; and not all, nor even any two of them, at the same time. He came *first* as "that *Prophet;*" He is *now* that *Priest,* and *will be* that *King* when He comes again. He finished His work as "that Prophet" before He became *that Priest;* and he finishes His work as *that Priest* before He will become *that King.*

And as He was, and as He is, and as He is to be, so our consideration of Him must be.

That is to say: When He was in the world as *that Prophet,* that is what the people were then to consider Him; and, as concerning that time, that is what we are now to consider Him. But they at that time could not consider Him as *that Priest,* nor, as concerning Him in that time, can we consider Him as *that Priest;* for when He was on earth, He was not a priest.

But when that time was past, He became Priest. He is now Priest. He is now just as truly Priest as, when He was on earth, He was *that Prophet.* And in his office and work of priest we are now to consider Him just as truly, just as thoroughly, and just as constantly that Priest, as, when He was on earth, they and we must consider Him as that Prophet.

And when He comes again in His glory and in the majesty of His kingdom, and upon the throne of His father David, then we shall consider Him as *that King,* which He will then indeed be.

But not until then can we truly consider Him in His kingly office, as He in that kingship and kingly office will be.

In His *kingly office* we can now truly contemplate Him as only that which He is yet to be. In His *prophetic office* we can now contemplate Him only as that which He has been. But in His *priesthood* we must now consider Him as that which He now is; for only that is what He now is. That is the office in which alone He is now manifested; and that is the office in which alone we can now actually consider Him in His own person and procedure.

Not only are His three offices of prophet, priest, and king successive, but they are successive for a purpose. And they are successive for a purpose in the exact order of the succession as given—prophet, priest and king. His office as prophet was preparatory and essential to His office as priest; and His offices of prophet and priest, in order, are preparatory to His office as king.

And to us the consideration of Him in these offices *in their order* is essential.

We must consider Him in His office as prophet, not only in order that we may be taught by Him who spake as never man spake, but also that we shall be able properly to consider Him in His office as priest.

And we must consider Him in His office as priest, not only that we may have the infinite benefit of His priesthood, but also that we shall be prepared for what we are to be. For it is written: "They shall be priests of God and of Christ, and shall reign with Him a thousand years." Rev. 20:6.

And having considered Him in His office of prophet as preparatory to our properly considering Him in His office as priest, it is essential that we consider Him in His office as priest in order that we shall be able to consider Him in His office as king; that is, in order that we shall be with Him there, and reign with Him there. For even of us it is written: "The saints of the Most High shall take the kingdom, and possess the kingdom forever, even forever and ever," and "they shall reign forever and ever." Dan. 7:18; Rev. 22:5.

His priesthood being the present office and work of Christ, this having been His office and work ever since His ascension to heaven, Christ in His priesthood is the all-important study for all Christians, as well as for all other people.

CHAPTER I

"Such an High Priest"

"Now of the things which we have spoken this is the sum: We have such an High Priest, who is set on the right hand of the throne of the Majesty in the heavens; a minister of the sanctuary, and of the true tabernacle, which the Lord pitched, and not man."

This is the summing up of the evidence of the high priesthood of Christ presented in the first seven chapters of Hebrews. The "sum" thus presented is not particularly that we have an High Priest, but that "we have *such* an High Priest." "Such" signifies "of that kind; of a like kind or degree,"—"the same as previously mentioned or specified; not another or different."

That is to say: In the preceding part (the first seven chapters of the epistle to the Hebrews) there have been specified certain things concerning Christ as High Priest, certain qualifications by which He became High Priest, or certain things which are becoming to Him as an High Priest, which are summed up in this text: "Now of the things which we have spoken this is the sum: We have *such* an High Priest."

It is necessary, therefore, to an understanding of this scripture that the previous portion of this epistle shall be reviewed to see what is the true weight and import of this word, "*such* an High Priest." The whole of the seventh chapter is devoted to the discussion of this priesthood. The sixth chapter closes with the thought of this priesthood. The fifth chapter is almost wholly devoted to the same thought. The fourth chapter closes with it; and the fourth chapter is but a continuation of the third chapter, which begins with an exhortation to "consider the Apostle and High Priest of our profession, Christ Jesus;" and this as the conclusion from what had already been presented. The second chapter closes with the thought of His being "a merciful and faithful High Priest;" and this also as the conclusion from what has preceded in the first and second chapters; for though they are two chapters, the *subject* is but one.

This sketch shows plainly that in the first seven chapters of Hebrews the one great thought over all is the priesthood of Christ; and that the truths presented, whatever the thought or the form may be, are all simply the presentation in different ways of the great truth of this priesthood; all of which is finally summed up in the words: "We have such an High Priest."

Therefore, in discovering the true weight and import of this expression, *"such an High Priest,"* it is necessary to begin with the very first words of the book of Hebrews, and follow the thought straight through to the summing up, bearing constantly in mind that the one transcendent thought in all that is presented is, *"such an High Priest;"* and that in all that is said, the one great purpose is to show to mankind that we have *"such* an High Priest." However rich and full may be the truths in themselves, concerning Christ, which are contained in the successive statements, it must be constantly borne in mind that these truths—however rich, however full,—are all expressed with the one great aim of showing that we have *"such* an High Priest." And in studying these truths as they are presented in the epistle, they must be held as subordinate and tributary to the great truth over all that is the "sum,"— "we have *such* an High Priest."

In the second chapter of Hebrews, as the conclusion of the argument there presented, it is written: "Wherefore in all things it behooved Him to be made like unto His brethren, that He might be a merciful and faithful *High Priest* in things pertaining to God." In this it is declared that Christ's condescension, his likeness to mankind, His being made flesh and dwelling amongst men, was necessary to His becoming "a merciful and faithful High Priest." But in order to know the measure of His condescension and what is the real meaning of His place in the flesh as the Son of man and man, it is necessary to know what was first the measure of His exaltation as the Son of God and God: and this is the subject of the first chapter.

The condescension of Christ, the position of Christ, and the nature of Christ as He was in the flesh in the world, are given in the second chapter of Hebrews more fully than in any other one place in the Scriptures. But this is in the *second* chapter. The first chapter precedes it. Therefore the truth and the thought presented in the first chapter are essentially precedent to the second chapter. The first chapter must be fully understood in order to be able to follow the thought and understand the truth in the second chapter.

In the first chapter of Hebrews, the exaltation, the position, and the nature of Christ as He was in heaven before He came to the world are more fully given than in any other single portion of the Scriptures. Therefore it is certain that an understanding of the position and nature of Christ as He was in heaven is essential to a proper understanding of His position and nature as He was on earth. And since it behooved Him to be what He was on earth, in order that He might be a merciful and faithful High Priest, it is essential to know what He was in heaven; for this is essentially precedent to what He was on earth, and is therefore an essential part of the evidence that is summed up in the expression, "We have *such* an High Priest."

CHAPTER II

Christ as God

WHAT, then, is the thought concerning Christ in the first chapter of Hebrews?

First of all there is introduced "God"—God the Father—as the speaker to men, who "in time past spake unto the fathers by the prophets;" and who "hath in these last days spoken unto us by His Son."

Thus is introduced Christ the Son of God. Then of Him and the Father it is written: "Whom He [the Father] hath appointed heir of all things, by whom also He [the Father] made the worlds." Thus, as preliminary to His introduction and our consideration of Him as High Priest, Christ the Son of God is introduced as being with God as Creator and as being the active, vivifying Word in the creation—"by whom also He [God] made the worlds."

Next, of the Son of God Himself, we read: "Who being the brightness of His [God's] glory, and the express image of His [God's] person ["the very impress of His substance," margin R. V.], and upholding all things by the word of His power, when He had by Himself purged our sins, sat down on the right hand of the Majesty on high."

This tells us that, in heaven, the nature of Christ was the nature of God; that He, in His person, in His substance, is the very impress, the very character, of the substance of God. That is to say that, in heaven, as He was before He came to the world, the nature of Christ was in very substance the nature of God.

Therefore it is further written of Him that He was "made so much better than the angels, as He hath by inheritance obtained a more excellent name than they." This more excellent name is the name "God," which, in the eighth verse, is given by the Father to the Son: "Unto the Son He [God] saith, Thy throne, O *God*, is forever and ever."

Thus, He is "so much" better than the angels as God is better than the angels. And it is because of this that He has that more excellent name,—the name expressing only what He *is,* in His very nature.

And this name "He hath by inheritance." It is not a name that was bestowed, but a name that is inherited.

Now it lies in the nature of things, as an everlasting truth, that the only name any person can possibly inherit is his father's name. This name, then, of Christ's, which is more excellent than that of the angels, is the name of His Father: and His Father's name is *God.* The Son's name, therefore, which He has by inheritance, is *God.* And this name, which is more excellent than that of the angels, is His because He is "so much better than the angels." That name being *God,* He is "*so much* better than the angels" as God is better than the angels.

Next, His position and nature, as better than that of the angels, is dwelt upon: "For unto which of the angels said He [the Father] at any time, Thou art My Son, this day have I begotten thee? And again, I will be to Him a Father, and He shall be to Me a Son?" This holds the thought of the more excellent name spoken of in the previous verse. For He, being the Son of God,—God being His Father,—thus hath "by inheritance" the name of His Father, which is God; and which is so much more excellent than the name of the angels, as God is better than they.

This is dwelt upon yet further: "And again, when He bringeth in the first begotten into the world, He saith, And let all the angels of God worship Him." Thus He is so much better than the angels that He is worshiped by the angels: and this according to the will of God, because He is, in His nature, God.

This thought of the mighty contrast between Christ and the angels is dwelt upon yet further: "Of the angels He saith, Who maketh His angels spirits, and His ministers a flame of fire. But unto the Son He saith, Thy throne, O *God*, is forever and ever ["from eternity to eternity," German translation]."

And again, "A scepter of righteousness is the scepter of Thy kingdom. Thou hast loved righteousness, and hated iniquity; therefore God, *even Thy* God, hath anointed Thee with the oil of gladness above Thy fellows."

And yet again, the Father, in speaking to the Son, says: "Thou,

Lord, in the beginning hast laid the foundation of the earth; and the heavens are the works of Thine hands: they shall perish; but Thou remainest; and they all shall wax old as doth a garment; and as a vesture shalt Thou fold them up, and they shall be changed: but Thou are the same, and Thy years shall not fail."

Note the contrasts here, and in them read the nature of Christ. The *heavens* shall *perish*, but *He remains*. The *heavens* shall *wax old*, but *His years* shall *not fail*. The *heavens* shall be *changed*, but *He* is *the same*. This shows that He is God: of the nature of God.

Yet more of this contrast between Christ and the angels: "To which of the angels said He at any time, Sit on My right hand, until I make thine enemies thy footstool? Are they not all ministering spirits, sent forth to minister for them who shall be heirs of salvation?"

Thus, in the first chapter of Hebrews, Christ is revealed higher than the angels, as God; and as *much* higher than the angels as is God, because He is God.

In the first chapter of Hebrews Christ is revealed as God, of the *name* of God, because He is of the *nature* of God. And so entirely is His nature of the nature of God, that it is the very impress of *the substance* of God.

This is Christ the Saviour, Spirit of Spirit, substance of substance, of God.

And this is essential to know in the first chapter of Hebrews, in order to know what is His nature revealed in the second chapter of Hebrews *as man*.

CHAPTER III

Christ as Man

CHRIST's likeness *to God,* as set forth in the first chapter of Hebrews, is only introductory to the setting forth of His likeness *to men,* as in the second chapter of Hebrews.

His likeness *to God,* as in the first chapter of Hebrews, is the only basis of true understanding of His likeness *to men,* as in the second chapter of Hebrews.

And this likeness *to God,* as given in the first chapter of Hebrews, is likeness,—not in the sense of a mere picture, or representation; but is *like*ness in the sense of being actually *like* in very nature,—the very "impress of His substance," Spirit of Spirit, substance of substance, of God.

And this is given as the preliminary to our understanding of His likeness *to men.* That is to say: from this we are to understand that His likeness to men is not merely in shape, in picture, or representation, but in *nature,* in *very substance.* Otherwise, the whole first chapter of Hebrews, with all its detail of information, is, in that connection, meaningless and misplaced.

What, then, *is* this truth of Christ made in the *like*ness of men, as given in the second chapter of Hebrews?

Bearing in mind, the great thought of the first chapter, and the first four verses of the second chapter,—of Christ in contrast with the angels, *higher* than the angels, *as God,*—we begin with the fifth verse of the second chapter, where begins the thought of Christ in contrast with the angels,—*lower* than the angels, *as man.*

So we read: "For unto the angels hath He not put in subjection the world to come, whereof we speak. But one in a certain place testified, saying, What is man, that Thou art mindful of him? or the son of man, that Thou visitest him? Thou madest him a little lower than the angels; Thou crownedst him with glory and honor, and didst set him over the works of Thy hands: Thou hast put all things in subjection under his feet. For in that He put all in subjection under Him, He left nothing that is not put under Him. But now we see not yet all things put under Him. But we see Jesus." Heb. 2:5–9.

That is to say: God has not put in subjection to the angels the world to come; but He *has* put it in subjection to *man:* yet *not* the man to whom it *was originally* put in subjection; for, though it *was* so, yet *now* we see it not so. The man lost his dominion, and, instead of having all things in subjection under his feet, he himself is now in subjection to death. And he is in subjection to death only because he is in subjection to sin; for "by one man sin entered into the world, and death by sin; and so death passed upon all men, for that all have sinned." Rom. 5:12. He is in subjection to death because he is in subjection to sin; for death is only the wages of sin.

Nevertheless, it stands eternally true that *not* unto the *angels* hath He put in subjection the world to come, but unto *man,* And, *now,* Jesus Christ is THE MAN.

For, though this dominion having been put in subjection to man, and though now we see it not so; though man was given the dominion over all, and now we see that dominion lost to that particular man; yet we *do* "see *Jesus,*" *as man,* come to regain that original dominion. We *do* "see Jesus" as *man,* come to have all things *put in subjection under Him.*

That man was the first Adam: this other Man is the last Adam. That first Adam was made a little lower than the angels: this last Adam, Jesus, also we see "made a little lower than the angels."

That first man did not remain in the position where he was *made,* "lower than the angels." He lost that, and went *still* lower, and became subject to sin; and, in that, subject to suffering, even to the suffering of death.

And the last Adam we see in *the same place,* in the *same condition:* "We see Jesus, who was *made a little lower than the angels* for the *suffering of death.*" And again: "Both he that sanctifieth and they who are sanctified are *all* OF ONE."

He which sanctifieth is Jesus. They who are sanctified are men of all nations, kindreds, tongues, and peoples. And *one* man sanctified, out of any nation, any kindred, any tongue, or any people, is divine demonstration that *every* soul of that nation, kindred, tongue, or people might have been sanctified. And Jesus, having become one of these, that He might bring them to glory, is proof that He is one of mankind altogether; that He, as man, and all men themselves, are "all of *one:* for which cause He is not ashamed to call them brethren."

Therefore, as *in heaven* He was higher than the angels, *as God;* so, on earth, He was lower than the angels, *as man.* As when He was higher than the angels, *as God,* He and God were *of one;* so when He was on the earth, lower than the angels, *as man,* He and man are *"of one."* So that, just as certainly as, on *the side of God,* Jesus and God are *of one*— of one Spirit, of one nature, of one substance; so *on the side of man,* Christ and man are *"of one"*—of one flesh, of one nature, of one substance.

The likeness of Christ *to God* is in *substance* as well as in form. And the likeness of Christ *to man* is in *substance* as well as in form. Otherwise, there is no meaning in the first chapter of Hebrews as introductory to the second chapter; no meaning in the antitheses between the first and second chapters; and the first chapter is out of place, and empty, as a basis of introduction to the second chapter.

CHAPTER IV

"He Took Part of the Same"

THE first chapter of Hebrews reveals that Christ's *like*ness to God is not simply in *form* or *representation*, but also in *very substance;* and the second chapter as clearly reveals that His *likeness* to men is not simply in form or in representation, but also in *very substance.* It is *likeness* to men *as they are* in *all things*, exactly *as they are.* Wherefore, it is written: "In the beginning was the Word, and the Word was with God, and the Word was God. . . . And *the Word* was *made flesh,* and dwelt among us." John 1:1–14.

And that this is *like*ness to man as he is in his fallen, sinful nature, and not as he was in his original, sinless nature, is made certain by the word: "We see Jesus, who was made a little lower than the angels *for* the *suffering of death."* Therefore, as man is *since he became subject to death, this* is what *we see Jesus* to be, in His place *as man.*

Therefore, just as certainly as we see Jesus lower than the angels, unto the suffering of death, so certainly it is by this demonstrated that, *as man,* Jesus took the nature of man *as he is since death entered;* and not the nature of man *as he was before* he became subject to *death.*

But death entered only because of sin: had not sin entered, death never could have entered. And we see Jesus made lower than the angels *for* the *suffering* of *death.* Therefore we see Jesus made in the nature of man, *as man is since* man sinned; and not as man was before sin entered. For this He did that He might *"taste death* for *every man."* In becoming man that He might reach man, He must come to man where man is. Man is subject to death. Therefore Jesus must become man, *as man is since he is subject to death.*

"For it became Him, for whom are all things, and by whom are all things, in bringing many sons unto glory, to make the captain of their salvation perfect through *sufferings.*" Heb. 2:10. Thus, in becoming man, it became Him to become such *as man is.* Man is subject to sufferings. Therefore it became Him to come to the man where he is, in his sufferings.

Before man sinned, he was not in any sense subject to sufferings. And for Jesus to have come in the nature of man as he was before sin entered, would have been only to come in a way and in a nature in which it would be impossible for Him to know the sufferings of man, and therefore impossible to reach him to save him. But since it became Him, in bringing men unto glory, to be made perfect through *suffering;* it is certain that Jesus, in becoming man, partook of the nature of man as he is since he became subject to suffering, even the suffering of death, which is the wages of sin.

And so it is written: "Forasmuch then as the children are partakers of flesh and blood, He also Himself likewise took part of *the same.*" Verse 14. He, in His human nature, took the same flesh and blood that men have. All the words that could be used to make this plain and positive are here put together in a single sentence.

The children of men are partakers of flesh and blood; and, because of this, *He* took part of the same.

But this is not all: He *also* took part of the same flesh and blood as that of which the children are partakers.

Nor is this all: He also *Himself* took part of the same flesh and blood as that of which the children of men are partakers.

Nor yet is this all: He also Himself *likewise* took part of the same flesh and blood as that of which men are partakers.

Thus the Spirit of inspiration so much desires that this truth shall be made so plain and emphatic as to be understood by all, that He is not content to use any fewer than all the words that could be used in the telling of it. And, therefore, it is declared that just as, and just as certainly as, "the children are partakers of flesh and blood, *He also Himself likewise* took part of *the same*" flesh and blood.

And this He did in order "that through death He might . . . deliver them who through fear of death were all their lifetime subject to bondage." He took part of the same flesh and blood as we have in the bondage of sin and the fear of death, in order that He might deliver us from the bondage of sin and the fear of death.

And so, "Both He that sanctifieth and they who are sanctified are all *of one:* for which cause He is not ashamed to call them *brethren.*"

This great truth of the blood-relationship, this blood-brotherhood, of Christ with men, is taught in the gospel *in Genesis.* For when God made His everlasting covenant with Abraham, the sacrifices were cut in two, and He, with Abraham, passed between the pieces. Gen. 15:8–18; Jer. 34; 18, 19; Heb. 7:5, 9. By this act the Lord entered into "the most solemn covenant known to the Oriental" or to all mankind,—the blood covenant,—and thus became blood-brother to Abraham, "a relation which outranks every other relation in life."

This great truth of Christ's blood-relationship to man is further taught in the gospel *in Leviticus.* In the gospel in Leviticus there is written the law of redemption of men and their inheritances. When any one of the children of Israel had lost his inheritance, or himself had been brought into bondage, there was redemption provided. If he was able of himself to redeem himself or his inheritance, he could do it. But if he was not able of himself to redeem, then the right of redemption fell to his nearest of kin in blood-relationship. It fell not merely to *one* who was *near* of kin among his brethren; but to *the* one who was *nearest* of kin, who was able. Lev. 25:24–28, 47–49; Ruth 2:20; 3:9, 12, 13; 4:1–14, with the marginal readings.

Thus in Genesis and Leviticus there has been taught through all these ages the very truth which we find here taught in the second chapter of Hebrews—the truth that man has lost his inheritance and is himself also in bondage. And as he himself can not redeem himself nor his inheritance, the right of redemption falls to the nearest of kin who is able. And *Jesus Christ* is the only one in all the universe who is able.

But to be the Redeemer He must be not only able, He must be a blood-relative. And He must also be not only *near* of kin, but the *nearest* of kin; and the nearest of kin by blood-relationship. Therefore, "as the children" of man—as the children of the one who lost our inheritance—"are partakers of *flesh and blood,* He also Himself likewise took part of the *same*"—took part of flesh and blood in very substance *like* ours, and so became our nearest of kin. And therefore it is written that He and we "are all *of one:* for which cause He is not ashamed to call us *brethren.*"

But the Scripture does not stop even yet with the statement of this all-important truth. It says, further: "For verily He took not on Him the nature of angels; but He took on Him the seed of Abraham. Wherefore in *all things* it behooved Him to be made *like* unto His brethren," whose blood-brother He became in the confirming of that everlasting covenant.

And this He did, in order that wherein "*He Himself* hath *suffered* being *tempted,* He *is able* to *succor* them that are *tempted.*" For He was "*touched* with the *feeling* of our infirmities;" being "in *all points tempted like as we are,* yet without sin." Heb. 4:15. Being *made* in His *human nature,* in all things *like* as *we are,* He could be, and He was, tempted in *all* points *like* as *we are.* The only way in which He could possibly be tempted "like as we are" was to become "*in all things*" "like as we are."

As in His human nature He is one of us, and as "Himself took our infirmities" (Matt. 8:17), He could be "touched with the *feeling* of our infirmities." Being in all things made *like* us, He, when tempted, felt just as we feel when we are tempted, and knows all about it: and so can help and save to the uttermost all who will receive Him. As in His flesh, and as in Himself in the flesh, He was as weak as we are, and of Himself could "do nothing" (John 5:30); so when He bore "our griefs, and carried our sorrows" (Isa. 53:4), and was tempted as we are, *feeling* as we *feel,* by His divine *faith* He conquered *all* by the *power of God which that faith brought to Him,* and which *in our flesh* He has *brought to us.*

Therefore, His name is called Immanuel, which is "God with us." Not God with *Him* only, but God with *us.* God was with *Him* in eternity, and could have been with Him even though He had not given Himself for us. But man through sin became without God, and God wanted to be again with us. Therefore *Jesus* became "*us,*" that God with *Him* might be "God with *us.*" And that is His *name,* because that is what he *is.* Blessed be His *name.*

And this is "the faith of Jesus" and the power of it. This is our Saviour: one of God, and one of man; and therefore able to save to the uttermost every soul who will come to God by Him.

CHAPTER V

"Made Under the Law"

"CHRIST JESUS, . . . being in the form of God, . . . emptied Himself, and took upon Him the form of a servant, and was made in the *likeness of men.*" Phil. 2:5–7, R. V. He was made in the likeness of men, as men are, just where they are.

"The Word was made flesh." He "took part of *the same*" flesh and blood as that of which the children of men are partakers, as they are *since man has fallen into sin.* And so it is written: "When the fulness of the time was come, God sent forth His Son, made . . . *under the law.*"

To be under the law is to be guilty, condemned, and subject to the curse. For it is written: "We know that what things soever the law saith, it saith to them who are under the law: that . . . all the world may become *guilty* before God." This, because "all have sinned, and come short of the glory of God." Rom. 3:19, 23; 6:14.

And the guilt of sin brings the curse. In Zech. 5:1–4, the prophet beheld a "flying roll; the length thereof . . . twenty cubits, and the breadth thereof ten cubits." The Lord said to him: "This is the curse that goeth forth over the face of the whole earth." And what is the cause of this curse over the face of the whole earth? This: "For every one that *stealeth* shall be cut off as on this side according to it; and every one that *sweareth* shall be cut off as on that side according to it."

That is, this roll is the law of God; one commandment being cited from each table, showing that both tables of the law are included in the roll. Every one that stealeth—every one that transgresseth the law in the things of the second table—shall be cut off as on *this side* of the law according to it; and every one that sweareth—every one that transgresseth in the things of the first table of the law—shall be cut off as on *that side* of the law according to it.

The heavenly recorders do not need to *write out* a statement of each particular sin of every man; but simply to indicate on the roll that pertains to each man the particular commandment that is violated in each transgression. And that such a roll of the law does go with every man wherever he goes, and even abides in his house, is plain from the next words: "I will bring it forth, saith the Lord of hosts, and it shall enter into the house of the thief, and into the house of him that sweareth falsely by My name: and it shall remain in the midst of his house."

And unless a remedy shall be found, there that roll of the law will remain until the curse shall consume that man, and his house, "with the timber thereof and the stones thereof:" that is, until the curse shall devour the earth in that great day when the very elements shall melt with fervent heat. For "the strength of sin" and the curse "is the law." 1 Cor. 15:56; Isa. 24:5, 6; 2 Peter 3:10–12.

But, thanks be to God, "God sent forth His Son, made . . . *under the law, to redeem them that were under the law.*" Gal. 4:4, 5. By His coming He brought redemption to every soul who is *under the law.* But in order perfectly to bring that redemption to men under the law, He Himself must come to men, just where they are, and as they are, *under the law.*

And this He did; for He was "made under the law;" He was made "guilty;" He was made condemned by the law; He was "made" as guilty as any man *is* guilty who is under the law. He was "made" under condemnation as fully as any man is under condemnation because of his violation of the law. He was "made" under the curse as completely as any man in the world has ever been, or ever can be, under the curse. For it is written: "He that is hanged ["on a tree"] is accursed of God." Deut. 21:23.

The Hebrew makes this stronger still; for the literal translation is: "He that hangeth on a tree is *the curse of God.*" And this is exactly the strength of the fact respecting Christ; for it is written that He was "made *a curse.*" Thus, when He was made under the law, He was made all that it means to be under the law. He was made guilty; He was made condemned; He was made a curse.

But bear in mind forever that all this "He *was made.*" He was *none of this* of *Himself,* of native fault; but all of it He "was *made.*" And He was made it all *for us:* for us who are *under the law:* for us who are *under condemnation* because of transgressions of the law: for us who are *under the curse* because of swearing, and lying, and killing, and stealing, and committing adultery, and all the other infractions of the roll of God's law that goeth with us and that remaineth in our house.

He was made under the law, *to redeem them that are under the law.* He was made a curse, *to redeem them that are under the curse* BECAUSE of being under the law.

But for whomsoever it was done, and whatsoever is accomplished by the doing of it, there must never be forgotten the *fact* that, in order to the doing of that which was done, He had to be "made" that which those *already were* for whom the thing was done.

Any man, therefore, in all the world, who knows guilt, by that very thing knows also what Jesus felt for him; and by this knows how close Jesus has come to him. Whosoever knows what is condemnation, in that knows exactly what Jesus felt for him; and so knows how thoroughly Jesus is able to sympathize with him and to redeem him. Whosoever knows the curse of sin, "the plague of his own heart," in that can know exactly what Jesus experienced for him; and how entirely Jesus identified Himself, in very experience, with him.

Bearing guilt, being under condemnation, and so under the weight of the curse, Jesus, *a whole lifetime in this world of guilt, condemnation, and the curse,* lived the perfect life of the righteousness of God, *without ever sinning at all.* And whenever any man knowing guilt, condemnation, and the curse of sin; and knowing that Jesus actually felt in His experience all this *just as man feels it;* then, *in addition,* that man, *by believing in Jesus,* can know in *his* experience the blessedness of the perfect life of the righteousness of God, in *his* life, to redeem *him* from guilt, from condemnation, and from the curse; and to be manifested in *his* whole lifetime to keep *him* from ever sinning at all.

Christ was made under the law, to redeem them that were under the law. And that blessed work is accomplished for every soul who accepts of that redemption.

"Christ hath redeemed us from the curse of the law, being made a curse for us." His being made a curse is not in vain: it accomplishes all that was intended by it, in behalf of every man who will receive it. For it was all done "that the blessing of Abraham might come on the Gentiles through Jesus Christ; that we might receive the promise of the Spirit through faith." Gal. 3:14.

Still, whatever was intended by it, and whatever is accomplished by it, there must always be borne in mind by every soul the FACT that, in His condescension, in His emptying Himself and being "made in the *likeness of men*," and *"made flesh,"* He was made under the law, guilty,—under condemnation, under the curse,—as really and as entirely as is any soul that shall ever be redeemed.

And having passed through it all, He is the author of eternal salvation, and is able to save to the uttermost from deepest loss all who come unto God by Him.

CHAPTER VI

"Made of a Woman"

By what means was Christ made flesh? Through what means was He partaker of human nature?—Exactly the same means as are all of us partakers: all of the children of men. For it is written: "As the children [of the man] are partakers of flesh and blood, He also Himself likewise took part of the same."

Likewise signifies "in the like way," "thus," "in the same way." So He partook of "the same" flesh and blood that men have, in *the same way* that men partake of it. Men partake of it by birth. So "likewise" did He. Accordingly, it is written, *"Unto us* a Child *is born."*

Accordingly, it is further written: "God sent forth His Son, *made of a woman."* Gal. 4:4. He, being made of a woman in *this world,* in the nature of things He was made of the only *kind* of woman that this world knows.

But why must He be made of a woman? why not of a man?— For the simple reason that to be made of a man would not bring Him close enough to mankind as mankind is, under sin. He was made of a woman in order that He might come, in *the very uttermost,* to where human nature is in its sinning.

In order to do this, He *must* be made of a woman; because *the woman,* not the man was *first,* and originally, *in the transgression.* For "Adam was not deceived, but the *woman* being deceived *was in the transgression."* 1 Tim. 2:14.

To have been made only of the descent of man would have been to come short of the full breadth of the field of sin; because the *woman had sinned,* and sin was thus *in the world, before* the *man sinned.*

Christ was thus made of a woman in order that He might meet the great world of sin at its very fountain head of entrance into this world. To have been made otherwise than of a woman would have been to come short of this, and so would have been only to miss completely the redemption of men from sin.

It was "the Seed of the woman" that was to bruise the serpent's head; and it was only as "the seed of the woman," and "made of a woman," that He could meet the serpent on his own ground, at the very point of the entrance of sin into this world.

It was the woman who, in this world, was originally in the transgression. It was the woman by whom sin originally entered. Therefore, in the redemption of the children of men from sin, He who would be the Redeemer must go *back of the man*, to meet the sin that was in the world *before* the *man* sinned.

This is why He, who came to redeem, was "made of a woman." By being made of a woman, He could trace sin to the very fountain head of its original entry into the world by the woman. And thus, in finding sin in the world, and uprooting it from the world, from its original entrance into the world till the last vestige of it shall be swept from the world, in the very nature of things, He must partake of human nature as it is since sin entered.

Otherwise, there was no kind of need whatever that He *should* be "made of a *woman*." If He were not to come into closest contact with sin as it is in the world, as it is in human nature; if He were to be removed one single degree from it as it is in human nature,—then He need not have been "made of *a woman*."

But as He was made of a woman,—not of a man; as He was made of the one by whom sin entered in its very origin into the world, and not made of the man, who entered into the sin after the sin had entered into the world,—this demonstrates beyond all possibility of fair question that between Christ and sin in this world, and between Christ and human nature as it is under sin in the world, there is no kind of separation, even to the shadow of a single degree. He was made flesh; He was made to be sin. He was made flesh as flesh is, and only as flesh is in this world; and was made to be sin only as sin is.

And this must He do to redeem lost mankind. For Him to be separated a single degree, or a shadow of a single degree, in any sense, from the nature of those whom He came to redeem, would be only to miss everything.

Therefore, as He was made "under the law," *because they are under the law* whom He would redeem; and as He was made a curse, *because they are under the curse* whom He would redeem; and as He was made sin, *because they are sinners,* "sold under sin," whom He would redeem,—precisely so He must be made flesh, and "the *same*" flesh and blood, *because they are flesh* and blood whom He would redeem; and must be made "of a woman," *because* sin was in the world *first* by and in the woman.

Consequently, it is true, without any sort of exception, that "*in all things* it behooved Him to be made like unto His brethren." Heb. 2:17.

If He were not of the same flesh as are those whom He came to redeem, then there is no sort of use of His being made flesh at all. More than this: Since the only flesh that there is in this wide world which He came to redeem, is just the poor, sinful, lost, human flesh that all mankind have; if this is not the flesh that He was made, then He never really came *to* the world which needs to be redeemed. For if He came in a human nature different from that which human nature in this world actually is, then, even though He were in the world, yet, for any practical purpose in reaching man and helping him, He was as far from him as if He had never come: for, in that case, in His human nature He was just as far from man and just as much of another world as if He had never come into this world at all.

It is thoroughly understood that in His birth Christ did partake of the nature of Mary—the "woman" of whom He was "made." But the carnal mind is not willing to allow that God in His perfection of holiness could endure to come to men where they are in their sinfulness. Therefore endeavor has been made to escape the consequences of this glorious truth, which is the emptying of self, by inventing a theory that *the nature of the virgin Mary* was *different* from the nature of the rest of mankind: that her flesh was not exactly such flesh as is that of all mankind. This invention sets up that, by some special means, Mary was made different from the rest of human beings, especially in order that Christ might be *becomingly* born of her.

This invention has culminated in what is known as the Roman Catholic dogma of the Immaculate Conception. Many Protestants, if not the vast majority of them as well as other non-Catholics, think that the Immaculate Conception refers to the *conception of Jesus* by the virgin Mary. But this is altogether a mistake. It refers not at all to the conception of Christ by Mary: but to the conception of *Mary herself* by *her* mother.

The official and "infallible" doctrine of the Immaculate Conception, as solemnly defined as an article of faith, by Pope Pius

IX, speaking *ex cathedra,* on the 8th of December, 1854, is as follows:—

By the authority of our Lord Jesus Christ, of the blessed apostles Peter and Paul, and by our own authority, we declare, pronounce, and define, that the *doctrine which holds* that the most blessed Virgin Mary, in the *first instant of* HER conception, *by a special grace and privilege* of Almighty God, *in view of the merits of Jesus Christ,* the Saviour of mankind, was *preserved free from all stain of original sin,* has been revealed by God, and, therefore, is to be firmly and steadfastly believed by all the faithful.

Wherefore, if any shall presume, which may God avert, to think in their heart otherwise than has been defined by us, let them know, and moreover understand, that they are condemned by their own judgment, that they have made shipwreck as regards the faith, and have fallen away from the unity of the Church.—*"Catholic Belief," page 214.*

This conception is defined by Catholic writers thus:—

The ancient writing, "De Nativitate Christi," found in St. Cyprian's works, says: Because (Mary) being *"very different* from *the rest of mankind,* human nature, *but not sin,* communicated itself to her."

Theodore, patriarch of Jerusalem, said in the second council of Nice, that Mary "is truly the mother of God, and virgin before and after childbirth; and she *was created* in a *condition more sublime* and *glorious* than that *of all natures,* whether intellectual or corporeal."—*Id., pages 216, 217.*

This plainly puts the nature of Mary entirely beyond any real likeness or relationship to mankind or human nature as it is. Having this clearly in mind, let us follow this invention in its next step. Thus it is, as given in the words of Cardinal Gibbons:—

We affirm that the Second Person of the Blessed Trinity, the Word of God, who in His divine nature is, from all eternity, begotten of the Father, consubstantial with Him, was in the fulness of time again begotten, by being born of the virgin, thus taking to himself from her maternal womb a human nature of *the same substance with hers.*

As far as the sublime mystery of the incarnation can be reflected in the natural order, the blessed Virgin, under the overshadowing of the Holy Ghost, by communicating to the Second Person of the adorable Trinity, as mothers do, a true human nature *of the same substance with her own,* is thereby really and truly His mother.—*"Faith of Our Fathers," pages 198, 199.*

Now put these two things together. First, we have the nature of Mary defined as being not only "very different from the rest of mankind," but "more sublime and glorious *than all natures:*" thus putting her infinitely beyond any real likeness or relationship to mankind as we really are.

Next, we have Jesus described as taking from her a human nature of the *same substance as hers.*

From this theory it therefore follows as certainly as that two and two make four, that in His human nature the Lord Jesus is "very different" from the rest of mankind: indeed, His nature is not human nature at all.

Such is the Roman Catholic doctrine concerning the human nature of Christ. The Catholic doctrine of the human nature of Christ is simply that that nature is not human nature at all, but divine: "more sublime and glorious than all natures." It is that in His human nature Christ was so far separated from mankind as to be utterly unlike that of mankind: that His was a nature in which He could have no sort of fellow-feeling with mankind.

But such is not the faith of Jesus. The faith of Jesus is that "as the children are partakers of flesh and blood, He also Himself likewise took part of *the same.*"

The faith of Jesus is that God sent "His own Son in the *likeness* of *sinful flesh.*"

The faith of Jesus is that "in *all things* it behooved Him to be *made like unto His brethren.*

The faith of Jesus is that He "Himself took our infirmities," and was touched "with the feeling of our infirmities," being tempted in *all* points *like as* we are. If He was not as we are, He could not possibly be tempted "like *as* we are." But He *was* "in all points tempted like as we are." Therefore He was "in all points" "like as we are."

In the quotations of Catholic faith which in this chapter we have cited, we have presented the faith of Rome as to the human nature of Christ and of Mary. In the second chapter of Hebrews and kindred texts of Scripture there is presented, and in these studies we have endeavored to reproduce as there presented, the faith of Jesus as to the human nature of Christ.

The faith of Rome as to the human nature of Christ and Mary, and of ourselves, springs from that idea of the natural mind that God is too pure and too holy to dwell with us and in us in our sinful human nature: that sinful as we are, we are too far off for Him in His purity and holiness to come to us just as we are.

The true faith—the faith of Jesus—is that, far off from God as we are in our sinfulness, in our human nature which He took, He *has come* to us just where we are; that, infinitely pure and holy as He is, and sinful, degraded, and lost, as we are, He in Christ by His Holy Spirit will willingly dwell with us and in us, to save us, to purify us, and to make us holy.

The faith of Rome is that we must be pure and holy in order that God shall dwell with us at all.

The faith of Jesus is that God must dwell with us, and in us, in order that we shall be holy or pure at all.

CHAPTER VII

The Law of Heredity

"The Word was made flesh."

"When the fulness of the time was come, God sent forth His Son, made of a woman." Gal. 4:4.

"And the Lord hath laid on Him the iniquity of us all." Isa. 53:6.

We have seen that, in His being made of a woman, Christ reached sin at the very fountain head of its entrance into this world; and that He must be made of a woman to do this. Also there was laid upon Him the iniquity, in the actual sins, of us all.

Thus all the sin of this world, from its origin in the world to the end of it in the world, was laid upon Him: both sin as it is in itself, and sin as it is when committed by us: sin in its *tendency,* and sin in the *act:* sin as it is hereditary in us, *uncommitted* by us; and sin as it is *committed* by us.

Only thus could it be that there should be laid upon Him the iniquity of *us all.* Only by His subjecting Himself to the law of heredity could He reach sin in full and true measure as sin truly is. Without this there could be laid upon Him our sins which have been *actually committed,* with the guilt and condemnation that belong to them. But, beyond this, there is in each person, in many ways, the *liability* to sin, *inherited* from generations back, which has not yet culminated in the act of sinning, but which is ever ready, when occasion offers, to blaze forth in the actual committing of sins. David's great sin is an illustration of this. Ps. 51:5; 2 Sam. 11:2.

In delivering us from sin, it is not enough that we shall be saved from the sins that we have actually committed: we must be saved from committing other sins. And that this may be so, there must be met and subdued this *hereditary liability* to sin; we must become possessed of power to keep us from sinning—a power to conquer this liability, this hereditary tendency that is in us, to sin.

All our sins which we have actually committed were laid upon Him, were imputed to Him, so that His righteousness may be laid upon us, may be imputed to us. *Also* our *liability to sin* was laid upon Him, in His being made flesh, in His being born of a woman, of the same flesh and blood as we are, so that His righteousness might be actually manifested in us as our daily life.

Thus He met sin *in the flesh which He took,* and *triumphed over it,* as it is written: "God sending His own Son in *the likeness of sinful flesh,* and for sin, *condemned sin* IN THE FLESH." And again: "He is our peace, . . . having abolished *in His flesh* the enmity."

And thus, just as our sins *actually committed* were imputed to Him, that His righteousness might be imputed to us; so His meeting and conquering, *in the flesh,* the *liability to sin,* and in that *same* flesh *manifesting righteousness,* enables us in Him, and Him in us, to meet and conquer in the flesh this *same liability to sin,* and to manifest righteousness in the same flesh.

And thus it is that for the sins which we have actually committed, for the sins that are past, *His righteousness* is imputed to *us,* as *our sins* were imputed to *Him.* And to *keep us from sinning,* His righteousness is *imparted* to us in our flesh; as our flesh, with its liability to sin, was *imparted* to Him. Thus He is the complete Saviour. He saves from all the sins that we have actually committed; and saves equally from all the sins that we might commit, dwelling apart from Him.

If He took not the same flesh and blood that the children of men have, with its liability to sin, then where could there be any philosophy or reason of any kind whatever in *His genealogy* as given in the Scriptures? He was descended from David; He was descended from Abraham; He was descended from Adam; and, by being made of a woman, He reached even back of Adam, to the beginning of sin in the world.

In that genealogy there are Jehoiakim, who for his wickedness was "buried with the burial of an ass, drawn and cast forth beyond the gates of Jerusalem" (Jer. 22:19); Manasseh, who caused Judah to do "worse than the heathen;" Ahaz, who "made Judah naked, and transgressed sore against the Lord;" Rehoboam, who was born of Solomon after Solomon turned from the Lord; Solomon himself, who was born of David and Bathsheba; there are also Ruth the Moabitess, and Rahab; as well as Abraham, Isaac, Jesse, Asa, Jehoshaphat, Hezekiah, and Josiah: the worst equally with the best. And the evil deeds of even the best are recorded equally with the good. And in this whole genealogy there is hardly *one*, whose life is written upon at all, of whom there is not some wrong act recorded.

Now it was at the end of such a genealogy as that that "the Word was *made flesh*, and *dwelt among us*." It was at the end of such a genealogy as that that He was "made of a woman." It was in such a line of descent as that that God sent "His own Son in *the likeness of sinful flesh*." And such a descent, such a genealogy, meant something to Him, as it does to every other man, under the great law that the iniquities of the fathers are visited upon the children, to the third and fourth generations. It meant everything to Him in the terrible temptations in the wilderness of temptation, as well as all the way through His life in the flesh.

Thus, both by heredity and by imputation, He was "laden with the sins of the world." And, thus laden, at this immense disadvantage, He passed triumphantly over the ground where, at no shadow of any disadvantage whatever, the first pair failed.

By His death He paid the penalty of all sins actually *committed*, and thus can justly bestow His righteousness upon all who choose to receive it. And by condemning sin *in the flesh*, by abolishing in His *flesh* the enmity, He delivers from the power of the law of heredity; and so can, in righteousness, impart His divine nature and power to lift above that law, and hold above it, every soul that receives Him.

And so it is written: "When the fulness of the time was come, God sent forth His Son, made of a woman, made under the law, to redeem them that were under the law, that we might receive the adoption of sons." Gal. 4:4. And "God sending His own Son in the likeness of sinful flesh, and for [on account of] sin, condemned sin in the flesh: that *the righteousness* of *the law* might be fulfilled *in us*, who walk not after the flesh, but after the Spirit." Rom. 8:3, 4. And "He is our peace, . . . having abolished in His flesh the enmity, . . . for to make in Himself of twain [God and man] one new man, so making peace." Eph. 2:14, 15.

Thus "*in all things* it behooved Him to be made like unto His brethren. . . . For in that He Himself hath suffered being tempted, He is able to succor them that are tempted."

Whether temptation be from within or from without, He is the perfect shield against it all; and so saves to the uttermost all who come unto God by Him.

God sending His own Son in the likeness of sinful flesh, Christ taking our nature as our nature is in its sinfulness and degeneracy, and God dwelling constantly with Him and in Him in that nature—in this God has demonstrated to all people forever, that there is no soul in this world so laden with sins or so lost that God will not gladly dwell with him and in him to save him from it all, and to lead him in the way of the righteousness of God.

And so certainly is his name Emmanuel, which is, *"God* with *us."*

CHAPTER VIII

"In All Things Like"

It should be particularly noted that in the first and second chapters of Hebrews the thought and discussion concerning the person of Christ is especially as to nature and *substance*. In Phil. 2:5–8, there is presented the thought of Christ's relationship to God and to man, especially as to nature and *form*. Thus: "Let this mind be in you, which was also in Christ Jesus: who, being in the *form* of *God*, thought it not robbery to be *equal with God:* but *emptied Himself*, and took upon Him the *form* of a *servant*, and was made in the likeness of men: and being found in *fashion* as a man, He humbled Himself, and became obedient unto death, even the death of the cross." Phil. 2:5–8, and R. V.

When Jesus emptied Himself He became man: and God was revealed in the Man. When Jesus emptied Himself, on the one side man appeared, and on the other side God appeared. Thus, in Him God and man meet in peace, and become one: "for He is our peace, who hath made both [God and man] one, . . . having abolished in His flesh the enmity, . . . to make in Himself of twain [God and man] one new man, so making peace." Eph. 2:14, 15.

He who was in the form of *God* took the form of *man*.

He who was equal with *God* became equal with *man*.

He who was *Creator* and *Lord*, became *creature* and *servant*.

He who was in the likeness of *God*, was made in the likeness of *men*.

He who was *God*, and *Spirit*, was made *man*, and *flesh*. John 1:1, 14.

Nor is this true only as to *form:* it is true as to *substance*. For, Christ was *like God* in the sense of being of the nature, in very substance, of God. He was made in the *like*ness of *men*, in the sense of being *like men*, in the nature and very substance of men.

36

Christ was God. He became man. And when He became *man,* He *was* man as really as He was God.

He became man in order that He might redeem man.

He came to man where man *is,* to bring man to Him where he *was* and *is.*

And in order to redeem man from what man is, He was *made* what *man is:*—

Man is flesh. Gen. 6:3; John 3:6. "And the Word was made flesh." John 1:14; Heb. 2:14.

Man is under the law. Rom. 3:19. Christ was "made under the law." Gal. 4:4.

Man is under the curse. Gal. 3:10; Zech. 5:1–4. "Christ was made a curse." Gal. 3:13.

Man is sold under sin (Rom. 7:14), and laden with iniquity. Isa. 1:4. And "the Lord hath *laid* on *Him* the iniquity of *us all.*" Isa. 53:6.

Man is "a body of sin." Rom. 6:6. And God "hath made Him to be *sin.*" 2 Cor. 5:21.

Thus, literally, "in *all things* it behooved Him to be made *like* unto His brethren."

Yet it must never be forgotten, it must be borne in mind and heart constantly and forever, that in none of this as to man, the flesh, sin, and the curse was Christ ever *of Himself* or of His own original nature or fault. All this He "was *made.*" "He *took upon* Him the form of a servant, and *was made* in the likeness of men."

And in all this *Christ* was *"made"* what, before, He *was not,* in order that *the man* might be made *now* and *forever* what he *is not.*

Christ was the Son of God. He became the Son of man, that the sons of men might become the sons of God. Gal. 4:4; 1 John 3:1.

Christ was Spirit. 1 Cor. 15:45. He became flesh in order that man, who is flesh, might become spirit. John 3:6; Rom. 8:8–10.

Christ, who was altogether of the *divine* nature, was made partaker of *human* nature, in order that we who are altogether of the *human* nature "might be partakers of the divine nature." 2 Peter 1:4.

Christ, who *knew no sin,* was *made to be sin,* even the sinfulness of man, in order that *we,* who knew no righteousness, might be made righteousness, even the righteousness of God.

And as the righteousness of God, which, in Christ, the *man* is *made,* is *real righteousness,* so the sin of men, which *Christ was made* in the flesh, was *real sin.*

As certainly as our sins, when upon us, are real sins to us, so certainly, when these sins were laid upon Him, they became real sins to Him.

As certainly as guilt attaches to these sins, and *to us* because of them, when they are *upon us*, so certainly this guilt attached to these same sins of ours, and *to Him* because of them, when they were laid *upon Him*.

As the sense of condemnation and discouragement of our sins was real to us, when these sins of ours were upon us, so certainly this same sense of condemnation and discouragement *because of the guilt of these sins* was *realized by Him* when these sins of ours were laid upon Him.

Thus the guilt, the condemnation, the discouragement of the knowledge of sin were His—were a fact in His conscious experience—as really as they were ever such in the life of any sinner that was ever on earth. And this awful truth brings to every sinful soul in the world the glorious truth that "the righteousness of God," and the rest, the peace, and the joy, of that righteousness, are a fact in the conscious experience of the believer in Jesus in this world, as really as they are in the life of any saint who was ever in heaven.

He who knew the height of the righteousness of God, acquired also the knowledge of the depth of the sins of men. He knows the awfulness of the depths of the sins of men, as well as He knows the glory of the heights of the righteousness of God. And by this "His knowledge shall My righteous Servant justify many." Isa. 53:11. By this His knowledge He is able to deliver every sinner from the lowest depths of sin, and lift him to the highest height of righteousness, even the very righteousness of God.

Made "in all things" like unto us, He *was* in all points like as we *are*. So fully was this so that He could say, even as we must say the same truth, "I can of Mine own self do nothing." John 5:30.

Of Him this was so entirely true that, in the weakness and infirmity of the flesh,—ours which He took—He *was* as *is* the man who is without God and without Christ. For it is only without Him that men can do nothing. *With* Him, and *through* Him, it is written: "I can do all things." But of those who are *without* Him, it is written: *"Without Me* ye can do *nothing."* John 15:5.

Therefore, when of Himself He said, "I can of Mine own self do nothing," this makes it certain forever that in the flesh,—because of our infirmities which He took; because of our sinfulness, hereditary and actual, which was laid upon Him, and imparted to Him;—He was of Himself in that flesh exactly as is the man who, in the infirmity of the flesh, is laden with sins, actual and hereditary, and who is without God. And standing thus weak, laden with sins, and helpless, as we are, in divine faith He exclaimed, "I will put My trust in Him." Heb. 2:13.

He came "to seek and to save that which was lost." And in saving the lost, He came to the lost where we are. He put Himself among the lost. "He was numbered with the transgressors." He was "made to be sin." And from the standpoint of the weakness and infirmity of the lost, He *trusted in God*, that He would deliver Him and save Him. Laden with the sins of the world, and tempted in all points like as we are, He hoped in God, and trusted in God to save Him from all those sins, and to keep Him from sinning. Ps. 69:1–21; 71:1–20; 22:1–22; 31:1–5.

And this is the faith of Jesus: this is the point where the faith of Jesus reaches lost, sinful man, to help him. For thus it has been demonstrated, to the very fulness of perfection, that there is no man in the wide world for whom there is not hope in God: no one so lost that he can not be saved by trusting God in this faith of Jesus. And this faith of Jesus, by which in the place of the lost, he hoped in God, and trusted God for salvation from sin, and power to keep from sinning,—this victory of His it is that has brought to every man in the world divine faith, by which every man can hope in God, and trust in God, and can find the power of God to deliver him from sin and to keep him from sinning. That faith which he exercised, and by which He obtained the victory over the world, the flesh, and the devil,—that faith is His free gift to every lost man in the world. And thus "this is the victory that overcometh the world, even our faith;" and this is the faith of which He is the Author and Finisher.

This is the faith of Jesus that is given to men. This is the faith of Jesus that must be received by men, in order for them to be saved. This is the faith of Jesus which, now in this time of the Third Angel's Message, must be received and *kept* by those who will be saved from the worship of the "beast and his image," and enabled to keep the commandments of God. This is the faith of Jesus referred to in the closing words of the Third Angel's Message: "Here are they that *keep* the commandments of God, and *the faith of Jesus.*"

And now of the things which *we* have spoken, *this is the sum: "We have* SUCH *an High Priest.*" All that we have thus found in the first and second chapters of Hebrews is the essential foundation and preliminary of His high priesthood. For "*in all things* it behooved Him to be made like unto His brethren, *that* [so that, in order that] *He might be a merciful and faithful High Priest* in things pertaining to God, to make reconciliation for the sins of the people. For in that He Himself hath suffered, being tempted, He is able to succor them that are tempted." Heb. 2:17, 18.

CHAPTER IX

Further Qualifications
of Our High Priest

SUCH is the thought of the first two chapters of Hebrews. And upon this the third chapter opens, or rather the one great thought continues, with the beautiful exhortation: "Wherefore, holy brethren, partakers of the heavenly calling, consider the Apostle and High Priest of our profession, Christ Jesus; who was faithful to Him that appointed Him." Having presented Christ in the flesh, as He was made "in all things" like the children of men, and our nearest of kin, we are now asked to consider Him in His faithfulness in that position.

The first Adam was not faithful. This last Adam "was faithful to Him that appointed Him, as also Moses was faithful in all His [God's] house. For this Man was counted worthy of more glory than Moses, inasmuch as He who hath builded the house hath more honor than the house. For every house is builded by some man; but He that built all things is God. And Moses verily was faithful in all His [God's] house, as a servant, for a testimony of those things which were to be spoken after; but Christ [was faithful] as a son over His own house; whose house are we, if we hold fast the confidence and the rejoicing of the hope firm unto the end."

Next is cited Israel, who came out of Egypt, who were not faithful; who failed of entering into God's rest, because they believed not in Him. Then upon this is the exhortation to *us to* *"fear* lest a promise being left us of entering into His rest, any of you should seem to come short of it. For unto us was the gospel preached, as well as unto them; but the word preached did not profit them, not being mixed with faith in them that heard it. For we which have believed do enter into rest," in believing in Him who gave Himself for our sins.

We enter into rest in the forgiveness of all our sins, through believing in Him who was faithful in every obligation and under every temptation of life. We also enter into rest and there abide, by being partaker of His faithfulness, in which and by which we also shall be faithful to Him who has appointed us. For in considering Him "the High Priest of our profession" in His faithfulness, we are ever to consider that "we have not an high priest which can not be touched with the feeling of our infirmities; but was in all points tempted like as we are, yet without sin." Heb. 4:15.

When we "have *not* an high priest which can *not* be touched with the feeling of our infirmities," we *have* an High Priest who *can* be touched with the feeling of our infirmities. And the way in which He can and is touched with the feeling of our infirmities is that He "was in all points tempted like as we are." There is not a point in which any soul can be tempted but that He has been exactly so tempted, and has felt the temptation as truly as any human soul can feel it. But, though He was in all points tempted like as we are, and felt the power of it as truly as any one can, yet in it all He was faithful; and through it all He passed "without sin." And by faith in Him—in this His faithfulness—every soul can meet all temptation and pass through it without sinning.

This is our salvation: for He was made flesh as man, and in all things it behooved Him to be made like unto His brethren, and to be tempted in all points like as we are, "*that He might be a merciful and faithful High Priest* in things pertaining to God." And this not only "to make reconciliation for the sins of the people," but also to "succor"—to run under, to run to the aid of, to assist and deliver from suffering—"them that are tempted." He is our merciful and faithful High Priest to succor—run under—us when we are tempted, to keep us from falling under the temptation, and so to keep us from falling under sin. He *"runs under"* us in our temptation, so we shall not *fall under* the temptation, but shall conquer it, and rise in victory over it, sinning not.

"Seeing then that we have a great High Priest, that is passed into the heavens, Jesus the Son of God, *let us hold fast our profession.*" Heb. 4:14. And also seeing that we have such an High Priest, "let us therefore come boldly unto the throne of grace, that we may obtain mercy, and find grace to help in time of need."

Further, in presenting for our consideration our High Priest in His faithfulness, it is written that "every high priest taken from among men is ordained for men in things pertaining to God, that he may offer both gifts and sacrifices for sins: *who can have compassion on the ignorant, and on them that are out of the way;* for that He Himself also is compassed with infirmity." Heb. 5:1, 2.

And this is why it is that in order that He should be a merciful and faithful high priest in things pertaining to God, and that He should bring many sons unto glory, it became Him, as the Captain of their salvation, to be "compassed with infirmity," to be tried by temptation, to be "a man of sorrows and acquainted with grief;" thus "in all things" to be made acquainted with human experience, so that He truly "can have compassion on the ignorant, and on them that are not of the way." In a word, in order that He might be "a merciful and faithful High Priest in things pertaining to God," it became Him to be made "perfect through sufferings."

"And no man taketh this honor [of high priesthood] unto himself, but *he that is called of God,* as was Aaron. *So* also *Christ glorified not Himself* to be made an High Priest; but He that said unto Him, Thou art My Son, to-day have I begotten Thee. As He saith also in another place, Thou art a Priest forever after the order of Melchisedec. Who in the days of His flesh, when He had offered up prayers and supplications with strong crying and tears unto Him that was able to save Him from death, and was heard in that He feared; though He were a Son, yet *learned He obedience* by the things *which He suffered;* and being made perfect [being tested to perfection in all points], He became the author of *eternal salvation* unto all them that obey Him; called of God an High Priest after the order of Melchisedec." Heb. 5:4–10.

"And inasmuch as not without an oath He was made Priest; for those priests [of the Levitical priesthood] were made without an oath; but this *with an oath* by Him that said unto Him, The Lord sware and will not repent, Thou art a Priest forever after the order of Melchisedec: by *so much* was Jesus made a surety of a better testament." Thus, above all others, *by the oath of God,* Jesus was made a Priest. Therefore, and "by *so much*" "we have *such* an High Priest."

And further, "They [of the order of Aaron] truly were many priests, because they were not suffered to continue by reason of death: but this man, because He continueth ever, hath an unchangeable priesthood." Heb. 7:23, 24. By the oath of God He is made a Priest forever. He is also made a Priest "after the power of an endless life." Heb. 7:16. Therefore "He continueth ever." And because He continueth ever, He hath an "unchangeable priesthood." And because of all this, "He is able also to save them to the uttermost that come unto God by Him, seeing He *ever liveth* to make intercession for them." Heb. 7:25. And "*we have such* an High Priest."

And "*such* an High Priest *became us,* who is holy, harmless, undefiled, separate from sinners, and made higher than the heavens; who needeth not daily, as those high priests, to offer up sacrifice, first for his own sins, and then for the people's; for this He did once, when He offered up Himself. For the law maketh men high priests which have infirmity; but the *word of the oath,* which was since the law, maketh the Son [High Priest], who is consecrated forevermore." Heb. 7:26, 27.

CHAPTER X

"The Sum"

AND, "now of the things which *we* have spoken, this is the sum: We have such an High Priest." And what is that of which this is "the sum"?

1. That He who was higher than the angels, as God, was made lower than the angels, as man.

2. That He who was of the nature of God was made of the nature of man.

3. That He who was in all things like God was made in all things like man.

4. That as man He was tempted in all points like as men are, and never sinned; but was in all things faithful to Him that appointed Him.

5. That, as man, tempted in all points like as we are, He was touched with the feeling of our infirmities, and was made perfect through sufferings, in order that He might be a merciful and faithful High Priest; and was called of God to be an High Priest.

6. That by the power of an endless life He was made High Priest.

7. And that by the oath of God He was made High Priest.

Such are the specifications of the Word of God, of which the "sum" is, "We have such an High Priest."

And yet that is only a part of "the sum." For the whole statement of "the sum" is, "We have such an High Priest, who is set on the right hand of the throne of the Majesty in the heavens; *a minister of the sanctuary,* and of *the true tabernacle,* which *the Lord pitched,* and not man."

On earth there was a sanctuary which man pitched, and which man made. True, this sanctuary was both made and pitched under the direction of the Lord; nevertheless, it is far different from the sanctuary and the true tabernacle which the Lord

Himself pitched, and not man—as far different as the work of man is from the work of God.

That "worldly sanctuary," with its ministry, is more briefly described, and the meaning of it is more briefly told, in Hebrews 9, than would be possible otherwise to do. Therefore we quote Heb. 9:2–12, inclusive: "For there was a tabernacle made; the first, wherein was the candlestick, and the table, and the shewbread; which is called the sanctuary. And after the second veil, the tabernacle which is called the holiest of all; which had the golden censer, and the ark of the covenant overlaid round about with gold, wherein was the golden pot that had manna, and Aaron's rod that budded, and the tables of the covenant; and over it the cherubims of glory shadowing the mercy-seat; of which we can not now speak particularly.

"Now when these things were thus ordained, the priests went always into the first tabernacle, accomplishing the service of God. But into the second went the high priest alone once every year, not without blood, which he offered for himself, and for the errors of the people; *the Holy Ghost this signifying,* that the way into the holiest of all was not yet made manifest, while as the first tabernacle was yet standing: which was a figure for the time then present, in which were offered both gifts and sacrifices, that could not make him that did the service perfect, as pertaining to the conscience; which stood only in meats and drinks, and divers washings, and carnal ordinances, imposed on them until the time of reformation. But Christ being come an High Priest of good things to come, by a greater and more perfect tabernacle, not made with hands, that is to say, not of this building; neither by the blood of goats and calves, but by His own blood He entered in once into the holy place, having obtained eternal redemption for us."

That sanctuary was but "a figure;" and it was but a figure "for the time then present." In it priests and high priests ministered and offered both gifts and sacrifices. But all this priesthood, ministry, gift, and sacrifice, was *equally with the sanctuary,* only "a figure for the time then present," for it all "could not make him that did the service perfect, as pertaining to the conscience."

That sanctuary and tabernacle itself was but a figure of the sanctuary and the true tabernacle which the Lord pitched, and not man.

The high priest of that sanctuary was but a figure of Christ, who is High Priest of the sanctuary and the true tabernacle.

The ministry of that high priest of the sanctuary on earth was but a figure of the ministry of Christ, our great High Priest, "who is set on the right hand of the throne of the Majesty in the heavens; a minister of the sanctuary, and of the true tabernacle, which the Lord pitched, and not man."

The offerings of the priesthood in the ministry of the sanctuary on earth were but a figure of the offering of Christ, the true High Priest, in His ministry in the sanctuary and the true tabernacle.

Thus Christ was the true substance and meaning of all the priesthood and service of the sanctuary on earth; and any part of it that ever passed without this as its meaning was simply meaningless. And as certainly as Christ is the true Priest of Christianity, of which the Levitical priesthood was a figure; so certainly the sanctuary of which Christ is minister is the true sanctuary of Christianity, of which the earthly sanctuary of the Levitical dispensation was a figure. And so it is written: "If *He were on earth,* He *should not be a priest,* seeing that there are priests that offer gifts according to the law: who serve unto *the example* and *shadow* of *heavenly things,* as Moses was admonished of God when he was about to make the tabernacle: for, See, saith He, that thou make all things according to *the pattern shewed to thee in the mount.*" Heb. 8:4, 5.

"It was therefore necessary that the *patterns of things in the heavens* should be purified with these [earthly sacrifices]; but the *heavenly things themselves* with *better sacrifices* than these. For Christ is not entered into the holy places made with hands, which are *the figures* of *the true;* but into *heaven itself,* now to appear in the presence of God for us." And in "heaven itself," in the Christian dispensation, there was seen the throne of God and a golden altar and an angel with a golden censer offering incense with the prayers of all saints, "And the smoke of the incense, which came with the prayers of the saints, ascended up before God out of the angel's hand." Rev. 4:5; 8:2–4. Also in this same time there was seen in "heaven itself" the temple of God; and "the temple of God was opened in heaven, and there was seen in His temple the ark of His testament." Rev. 11:19; 15:5–8; 16:1. And further there was seen there "seven lamps of fire burning before the throne." Rev. 4:5. There, too, was seen one like the Son of man clothed in the high priestly garment. Rev. 1:13.

There is therefore a Christian sanctuary, of which the former sanctuary was a figure, as truly as there is a Christian high priesthood of which the former high priesthood was a figure. And there is a ministry of Christ, our High Priest, in this Christian sanctuary, as truly as there was a ministry of the former priesthood in the former and earthly sanctuary. And "of the things which we have spoken, this is the sum: We have such an High Priest, who is set on the right hand of the throne of the Majesty in the heavens; a minister of the sanctuary and of the true tabernacle, which the Lord pitched, and not man."

CHAPTER XI

"That I May Dwell Among Them"

WHEN the Lord gave to Israel the original directions for the making of the sanctuary, that was to be a figure for the time then present, he said, "Let them make me a sanctuary, that I may dwell among them." Ex. 25:8.

That he might "dwell among them" was the object of the sanctuary. This purpose of the sanctuary is more fully stated in the following: "And there I will meet with the children of Israel, and the tabernacle [*margin*, "Israel"] shall be sanctified by my glory. And I will sanctify the tabernacle of the congregation, and the altar: I will sanctify also both Aaron and his sons, to minister to me in the priest's office. And *I will dwell among* the children of Israel, and will be their God. And they shall know that I am the Lord their God, that brought them forth out of the land of Egypt, *that I may dwell among them:* I am the Lord their God." Ex. 29:43–46; also Lev. 26:11, 12.

This purpose was not that he should dwell among them simply and only by the tabernacle's being set up in the midst of the camp of Israel. This is the great mistake that Israel made in the use of the tabernacle, and so almost wholly lost the true purpose of the sanctuary. When the tabernacle was made and was set up in the midst of the camp of Israel, many of the children of Israel supposed that that was enough; they supposed that to be the way in which God would dwell in the midst of them.

It is true that by the Shekinah, God did dwell in the sanctuary. But even the sanctuary with its splendid furniture, standing in the midst of the camp—this was not all of the sanctuary. In addition to the splendid building and its furniture, there were the sacrifices and offerings of the people; and the sacrifices and offerings on behalf of the people. There were the priests in their continual services; and there was the high priest in his holy ministry. Without these the sanctuary was for Israel practically an empty thing, even though the Lord did dwell in it.

And what was the meaning and purpose of these things? Let us see: When any of the children of Israel had "done somewhat against any of the commandments of the Lord concerning things which should not be done," and so was "guilty;" then "of his own voluntary will" he brought to the door of the tabernacle, his sacrificial lamb. Before the lamb was offered in sacrifice the individual who had brought it laid his hands upon its head and confessed his sins, and it was "accepted for him to make atonement for him." Then he who had brought the lamb and confessed his sins, slew it. Its blood was caught in a basin. Some of the blood was "sprinkled round about upon the altar of burnt offering," which was at the door of the tabernacle; some of it was put "upon the horns of the altar of sweet incense, which is in the tabernacle of the congregation;" some of it was sprinkled "seven times before the Lord before the vail of the sanctuary;" and all the rest of it was poured out "at the bottom of the altar of the burnt offering, which is at the door of the tabernacle of the congregation." The lamb itself was burnt upon the altar of burnt offering. And of all this service, it is written in conclusion: "and the priest shall make an atonement for his sin that he hath committed, and it shall be forgiven him." The service was similar in case of the sin and confession of the whole congregation. Also there was a similar service, a continual service morning and evening, in behalf of the whole congregation. But whether the services were individual or general, the conclusion of it was always declared to be "The priest shall make an atonement for him [or them], and it shall be forgiven him." See Leviticus chapters 1 to 5.

The course of service of the sanctuary was completed annually. And the day of the completion of the service, the tenth day of the seventh month, was especially "the day of atonement," or the cleansing of the sanctuary. On that day service was concluded in the Most Holy place. That day was the "once every year" when "the High Priest alone" went into the "Holiest of all" or Most Holy place. And, of the high priest and his service that day it is written, "He shall make an atonement for the holy sanctuary, and he shall make an atonement for the tabernacle of the congregation, and for the altar, and he shall make an atonement for the priests, and for all the people of the congregation." Lev. 16:2–34; Heb. 9:2–8.

Thus the services of the sanctuary, in the offering of the sacrifices and the ministering of the priests, and of the high priests alone, was for the making of atonement, and for the forgiveness and sending away of the sins of the people. Because of the sin and guilt, because of their having "done somewhat against any of the commandments of the Lord concerning things which should not be done," atonement must be made and forgiveness obtained. Atonement is literally at-one-ment. The sin and the guilt had separated them from God. By these services they were made at-one with God. Forgive is literally give-for. To forgive sin is to give for sin. Forgiveness of sin comes alone from God. What does God give, what has He given, for sin? He gave Christ, and Christ "gave himself for our sins." Gal. 1:4; Eph. 2:12–16; Rom. 5:8–11.

Therefore when an individual or the whole congregation of Israel had sinned and desired forgiveness the whole problem and plan, of forgiveness, of atonement, of salvation, was worked out before their faces. The sacrifice which was brought was in faith of the sacrifice which God had already made in giving His Son for sin. In this faith sinners were accepted of God, and Christ was received of them for their sin. Thus they were made at one with God; and thus God would dwell *in the midst of them:* that is He would dwell in each heart and abide in each life, to make that heart and life "holy, harmless, undefiled, and separate from sinners." And the placing of the tabernacle in the *midst of the camp* of Israel was an illustration, an object lesson and suggestion, of the truth that He would dwell in *the midst* of each individual. Eph. 3:16–19.

Some of that nation, in every age, saw in the sanctuary this great saving truth. But as a body, in all ages, Israel missed this thought; and stopping only with the thought of His dwelling *in the tabernacle* in the midst of the camp, they came short of having His own personal presence dwelling *in their individual lives.* Accordingly their worship became only outward and formal, rather than inward and spiritual. Therefore their own lives continued unreformed and unholy; and so those who came out of Egypt missed the great thing which God had for them, and "fell in the wilderness." Heb. 3:17–19.

The same mistake was made by the people after they had passed into the land of Canaan. They put their dependence on the Lord, *only as He dwelt in the tabernacle;* and would not allow that the tabernacle and its ministry should be the means of His

4157

dwelling in themselves through faith. Consequently their lives only increased in wickedness. Therefore God allowed the tabernacle to be destroyed and the ark of God to be taken captive by the heathen, (Jer. 7:12; 1 Sam. 4:10–22) in order that the people might learn to see and find and worship God individually, and so find Him to dwell with them individually.

After the absence of the tabernacle and its service from among Israel for about a hundred years, it was restored by David and was merged in the grand temple that was built by Solomon. But again its true purpose was gradually lost sight of. Formalism with its attending wickedness more and more increased, until in Israel the Lord was compelled to cry out: "I hate, I despise your feast days, and I will not smell in your solemn assemblies. Though ye offer Me burnt offerings and your meat offerings, I will not accept them: neither will I regard the peace offerings of your fat beasts. Take thou away from me the noise of thy songs; for I will not hear the melody of thy viols. But let judgment run down as waters, and righteousness as a mighty stream." Amos 5:21–24.

Also in Judah, by Isaiah, He was compelled to make a like plea: "Hear the word of the Lord, ye rulers of Sodom; give ear unto the law of our God, ye people of Gomorrah. To what purpose is the multitude of your sacrifices unto Me? saith the Lord: "I am full of the burnt offerings of rams, and the fat of fed beasts; and I delight not in the blood of bullocks, or of lambs, or of he goats. When ye come to appear before Me, who hath required this at your hand, to tread My courts? Bring no more vain oblations; incense is an abomination unto Me; the new moons and sabbaths, the calling of assemblies, I can not away with; it is iniquity, even the solemn meeting. Your new moons and your appointed feasts My soul hateth: they are a trouble unto Me; I am weary to bear them. And when ye spread forth your hands, I will hide Mine eyes from you: yea, when ye make many prayers, I will not hear: your hands are full of blood. Wash you, make you clean; put away the evil of your doings from before Mine eyes; cease to do evil; learn to do well; seek judgment, relieve the oppressed, judge the fatherless, plead for the widow. Come now, and let us reason together, saith the Lord: though your sins be as scarlet, they shall be as white as snow; though they be red like crimson, they shall be as wool." Isa. 1:10–18.

Yet His pleas were not regarded. Israel was therefore carried captive and her land was left desolate because of their wickedness; and the like fate hung over Judah. And still this danger to Judah was from the same great cause that the Lord had been striving always to teach the nation, and which they had not yet learned: the holding of *the temple,* and God's presence *in that temple,* as the great end; instead of holding that as only the means to the true end which was that *by means of the temple and its ministry* in accomplishing forgiveness and atonement, He who dwelt *in the temple* would dwell *in themselves.* And so again the Lord pleaded with His people by Jeremiah that He might save them from this mistake; and have them see and receive the great truth of the real meaning and purpose of the temple and its service.

Thus He said: "Behold, ye trust in lying words, that can not profit. Will ye steal, murder, and commit adultery, and swear falsely, and burn incense unto Baal, and walk after other gods whom ye know not; and come and stand before Me in this house, which is called by My name, and say, We are delivered to do all these abominations? Is this house, which is called by My name, become a den of robbers in your eyes? Behold, even I have seen it, saith the Lord.

"But go ye now unto My place which was in Shiloh, where I set My name at the first, and see what I did to it for the wickedness of My people Israel. And now, because ye have done all these works, saith the Lord, and I spake unto you, rising up early and speaking, but ye heard not; and I called you, but ye answered not; therefore will I do unto this house, which is called by My name, wherein ye trust, and unto the place which I gave to you and to your fathers, as I have done to Shiloh. And I will cast you out of My sight, as I have cast out all your brethren, even the whole seed of Ephraim. Therefore pray not thou for this people, neither lift up cry nor prayer for them, neither make intercession to Me: for I will not hear thee. . . . Oh that My head were waters, and Mine eyes a fountain of tears, that I might weep day and night for the slain of the daughter of My people! Oh that I had in the wilderness a lodging place of wayfaring men; that I might leave My people, and go from them! for they be all adulterers, an assembly of treacherous men. And they bend their tongues like their bow for lies: but they are not valiant for the truth upon the earth; for they proceed from evil to evil, and they know not Me. Jer. 7:8–16; 9:1, 3.

What were specifically the "lying words" in which these people trusted? Here they are: "Trust ye not in lying words, saying, The temple of the Lord, The temple of the Lord, The temple of the Lord, are these." Jer. 7:4. Thus it is made perfectly plain that the people though going through the forms of worship and of the temple service, went through all this merely as forms, missing entirely the purpose of the temple and its services, which was solely that God might reform and make holy the lives of the people by His dwelling in them individually. And missing all this, the wickedness of their own hearts only more and more made itself manifest. For this reason all their sacrifices, worship, and prayers, were only mockery and noise, so long as their hearts and lives were unreformed and unholy.

Therefore the word "came to Jeremiah from the Lord, saying, Stand in the gate of the Lord's house, and proclaim there this word, and say, Hear the word of the Lord, all ye of Judah, that enter in at these gates to worship the Lord. Thus saith the Lord of hosts, the God of Israel, Amend your ways and your doings, and I will cause you to dwell in this place. Trust yet not in lying words, saying, The temple of the Lord, The temple of the Lord, The temple of the Lord, are these. For if ye throughly amend your ways and your doings; if ye throughly execute judgment between a man and his neighbor; if ye oppress not the stranger, the fatherless, and the widow, and shed not innocent blood in this place, neither walk after other gods to your hurt: then will I cause you to dwell in this place, in the land that I gave to your fathers, forever and ever." Jer. 7:1–7.

Instead of allowing God's great purpose of the temple and its services to be met in themselves, the people utterly perverted that purpose. Instead of allowing the temple and its services which God in His mercy had planted among them, to teach them how that He in truth would dwell among them by dwelling in their hearts and making holy their lives, they excluded all this true purpose of the temple and its services and perverted it all to the utterly false purpose of sanctioning grossest wickedness and cloaking deepest, darkest unholiness.

For such a system there was no remedy but destruction. Accordingly the city was besieged and captured by the heathen. The temple, their "holy and beautiful house" was destroyed. And with the city and the temple a heap of burnt and blackened ruins, the people were carried captive to Babylon, where in their sorrow and the deep sense of their great loss they sought and found and worshiped the Lord in a way that so reformed their lives that if they had done it when the temple stood, it would have stood forever. Ps. 137:1–6.

God brought them back from Babylon a humbled and reformed people. His holy temple was rebuilt and its services were restored. The people again dwelt in their city, and their land. But apostasy again ensued. The same course was again repeated until, when Jesus, the great center of the temple and its services came to His own, the same old condition of things again prevailed. Matt. 21:12, 13; 23:13–32. In their hearts they could persecute and pursue Him to the death, and yet outwardly be so holy (?) that they could not cross the threshold of Pilate's judgment hall "lest they should be defiled"! John 18:28.

And the Lord's appeal to the people was still the same as of old—that they should find in their own personal lives the meaning of the temple and its services, and so be saved from the fate which had overtaken their nation through all its history, because of this same great mistake which they were repeating. Accordingly, one day in the temple Jesus said to the multitude there present, "Destroy this temple, and in three days I will raise it up. Then said the Jews, Forty and six years was this temple in building, and wilt thou rear it up in three days? But He spake of the temple of His body." John 2:19–21. When Jesus *in the temple* spoke thus to that people, referring to "the temple of His body" he was still endeavoring, as through all their history, to get them to perceive that the great purpose of the temple and its services always was that by means of the ministry and service there conducted, God would dwell and walk *in themselves* as He dwelt in the temple; making holy His dwelling-place in themselves, as His dwelling in the temple made that place holy: so that their bodies should be truly temples of the living God, because of God's dwelling in them and walking in them. 2 Cor. 6:16; 1 Cor. 3:16, 17; Lev. 26:11, 12; 2 Sam. 7:6, 7.

And still they would not see this truth. They would not be reformed. They would not have the purpose of the sanctuary met in themselves, that God should dwell in them. They rejected Him who came personally to show to them this true purpose and the true Way. Therefore again there was no remedy but destruction. Again their city was taken by the heathen. Again the temple, their "holy and beautiful house," was burned with fire. Again they were taken captive and were forever scattered, to be only "wanderers among the nations." Hosea 9:17.

Again let it be emphasized that the earthly sanctuary, the earthly temple, with its ministry and services, was *as such* only a figure of the true, which with *its* ministry and services was then in heaven. When the thought of the sanctuary was first presented to Moses for Israel it was stated by the Lord to him, "See . . . that thou make all things according to *the pattern* shewed to thee in the mount." Heb. 8:5; Ex. 25:40; 25:30; 27:8. The sanctuary on the earth was therefore a figure of the true, in the sense of its being *a pattern* of the true. The ministry and services in the earthly were "figures of the true" in the sense of being "the patterns" of the true—"the patterns of things in the heavens." Heb. 9:23, 24.

The true sanctuary of which this was a figure, the original of which this was a pattern, was then in existence. But in the darkness and confusion of Egypt, Israel had lost the true idea of this, as they had also of many other things which were plain to Abraham and Isaac and Jacob; and by this object-lesson God would give to them the knowledge of the true. It was therefore not a figure in the sense of being a type of something to come that did not yet exist; but a figure in the sense of being an object-lesson and *visible representation* of that which then existed but was *invisible,* to train them up to such an experience in faith and true spirituality that they should see the invisible.

And by all this God was revealing to them and to all people forever that it is by the priesthood, ministry, and service of Christ in the true sanctuary or temple which is in heaven, that He dwells amongst men. He was revealing that in this faith of Jesus, forgiveness of sins and atonement is ministered to men, so that God dwells in them and walks in them, He being their God and they His people; and thus they be separated from all the people that are upon the face of the earth—separated unto God as His own true sons and daughters to be built up *unto perfection* in the knowledge of God. Ex. 33:15, 16; 2 Cor. 6:16–18; 7:1.

CHAPTER XII

Perfection

THE great thought and purpose of the true sanctuary, its priesthood, and ministry, is that God shall dwell in the hearts of the people. What now is the great thought and purpose of His dwelling in the hearts of the people? The answer is, Perfection; the moral and spiritual perfection of the worshiper.

Let us consider this: At the close of the fifth chapter of Hebrews, immediately following the statement that Christ, "being made perfect, He became the Author of eternal salvation unto all them that obey Him; called of God an High Priest after the order of Melchisedec," it is written: "Therefore," that is, *because of this,* for *this reason,* "leaving the principles of the doctrine of Christ, *let us go on* unto *perfection.*" Heb. 6:1.

Next it is shown that perfection is attained only through the Melchisedec priesthood. And it is shown that this was always so, and that the Levitical priesthood was only temporary, and typical of the Melchisedec priesthood. Following this, in discussing the Levitical priesthood, it is written: "If therefore *perfection* were by the Levitical priesthood, . . . what further need was there that another priest should rise after the order of Melchisedec, and not be called after the order of Aaron?" Heb. 7:11. And again, in the same connection, "For the law made *nothing perfect,* but the bringing in of a better hope *did* [or "but it was the bringing in of a better hope," margin]; by the which we draw nigh unto God." Verse 19.

By these scriptures it is perfectly plain that the perfection of the worshiper is that which is offered and which is attained in the priesthood and ministry of Christ.

Nor yet are these all the words on this thought. For, as already quoted in the description of the sanctuary and its service, it is said that it "was a figure for the time then present, in which were

57

offered both gifts and sacrifices, that *could not make him* that did the service *perfect,* as pertaining to the conscience." That none of this could make him that did the service *perfect* is its great lack. Therefore that the priesthood and ministry of Christ in the true sanctuary, *can* and *does* make *perfect* him who enters by faith into the service, is the great thought and the goal of all.

That earthly service "could not make him that did the service perfect, as pertaining to the conscience." "But Christ being come an High Priest of good things to come, by a greater and more perfect tabernacle, not made with hands, that is to say, not of this building; neither by the blood of goats and calves, but by His own blood He entered in once into the holy place, having *obtained eternal redemption* for us." Heb. 9:11, 12. This sanctuary, priesthood, sacrifice, and ministry of Christ's does *make perfect* in *eternal redemption* every one who by faith enters into the service, and so receives that which that service is established to give.

Further, "For if the blood of bulls and of goats, and the ashes of an heifer sprinkling the unclean, sanctifieth to the purifying of the flesh: *how much more* shall the blood of Christ, who through the eternal Spirit offered Himself without spot to God, *purge your conscience* from dead works to serve the living God?" The blood of bulls and of goats and the ashes of an heifer sprinkling the unclean in the Levitical service and the worldly sanctuary *did* sanctify to the purifying of the flesh: for so the word concerning it continually declares. And that being so, "*how much more* shall the *blood of Christ,* who through the eternal Spirit offered Himself without spot to God," sanctify to the purifying *of the spirit* and "purge your conscience from dead works to serve the living God."

What are dead works? Death itself is the consequence of sin. Dead works therefore are works that have sin in them. Then the purging of the conscience from dead works is the so entirely cleansing of the soul from sin, by the blood of Christ, through the eternal Spirit, that in the life and works of the believer in Jesus sin shall have no place; the works shall be only works of faith, and the life shall be only the life of faith, and so be only the true and pure "service of the living God."

Again it is written: "The law having a shadow of good things to come, and not the very image of the things, *can never* with *those sacrifices* which they offered year by year continually *make the comers* thereunto *perfect.* For then would they not have ceased to be offered? because that the worshipers once purged should have had *no more conscience of sins.* But in those sacrifices there is a remembrance again made of sins every year. For it is *not possible* that the blood of bulls and of goats should *take away sins.*" Heb. 10:1–4.

This again shows that though *perfection* was the aim in all the ministry that was performed under the law, yet perfection was not attained by any of those performances. They were all simply figures for the time then present of the ministry and priesthood by which perfection *is* attained; that is the ministry and priesthood of Christ. Those sacrifices could not make the comers thereunto perfect. The true sacrifice and the true ministry in "the sanctuary and the true tabernacle" do make the comers thereunto *perfect:* and this perfection consists in the worshipers having "no more conscience of sins."

But since it is "not possible" for the blood of bulls and goats to take away sins, it was *not possible,* though those sacrifices were offered year by year continually, *so to purge the worshipers* that they should have *no more conscience of sins.* The blood of bulls and of goats, and the ashes of an heifer sprinkling the unclean could and did sanctify to the purifying of the flesh; but of the flesh only: and even this was "but a figure for the time then present" of "the blood of Christ," which *so much more* purges the worshipers that they have *no more conscience of sins.*

"Wherefore when He cometh into the world, He saith, Sacrifice and offering Thou wouldst not, but a body hast Thou prepared Me: in burnt offerings and sacrifices for sin thou hast had no pleasure. Then said I, Lo, I come . . . to do Thy will, O God. Above when he said, Sacrifice and offering and burnt offerings and offering for sin Thou wouldest not, neither hadst pleasure therein; which are offered by the law; then said He, Lo, I come to do Thy will, O God. *He taketh away the first,* that *He may establish the second.*" Heb. 10:5–9.

Here are mentioned two things: "the first," and "the second." What are these two things? Which is "the first," and which "the second"? The two things mentioned are sacrifice, offering, burnt offerings, and offering for sin—all as one; and the will of God. Sacrifice, offering, burnt offerings, and offering for sin—all as one—are "the first:" and "the will of God" is "the second." "He taketh away the first, that He may establish the second." That is, He taketh away sacrifice, offering, burnt offerings, and offering for sin, that He may establish *the will of God.* And the will of God is "even your sanctification" and your perfection. 1 Thess. 4:3; Matt. 5:48; Eph. 4:8, 12, 13; Heb. 13:20, 21. But this could never be accomplished by those sacrifices, offerings, burnt offerings, and offering for sin which were offered by the Levitical priesthood—they could not make the comers thereunto perfect. They could not so purge the worshipers that they should have no more conscience of sin. For it is not possible that the blood of bulls and of goats should take away sin.

Therefore, since the will of God is the sanctification and the perfection of the worshipers; since the will of God is that His worshipers shall be so cleansed that they shall have no more conscience of sin; and since the service and the offerings in that earthly sanctuary could not do this; He took it all away that He may establish the will of God. "*By the which* will *we are sanctified* through the offering of the body of Jesus Christ once for all."

The will of God is "even your sanctification." Sanctification is the true keeping of all the commandments of God. In other words, this is to say that the will of God concerning man is that His will shall be perfectly fulfilled in man. His will is expressed in His law of ten commandments, which is "the whole duty of man." This law is perfect, and perfection of character is the perfect expression of this law in the life of the worshiper of God. By this law is the knowledge of sin. And all have sinned and have come short of the glory of God; have come short of this perfection of character.

The sacrifices and the service in the earthly sanctuary could not take away the sins of men, and so could not bring them to this perfection. But the sacrifice and the ministry of the true High Priest in the sanctuary and the true tabernacle *do accomplish this.* This does take away utterly every sin. And the worshiper is so truly purged that he has no more conscience of sins. By the sacrifice, the offering, and the service of Himself, Christ took away the sacrifices and the offerings and the service which could never take away sins; and by His perfect doing of the perfect will of God He established the will of God. "By the which will *we* are sanctified through the offering of the body of Jesus Christ once for all." Heb. 10:10.

In that former earthly sanctuary and service, "every priest standeth daily ministering and offering oftentimes the same sacrifices, which *can never take away sins.*" But in the service in the sanctuary and the true tabernacle, "this Man, after He had offered one sacrifice for sins forever, sat down on the right hand of God; from henceforth expecting till His enemies be made His footstool. For by *one offering* He *hath perfected forever* them that are sanctified." Heb. 10:11–14.

Thus perfection in every respect is attained through the priesthood, the sacrifice, and the service of this our great High Priest at the right hand of the throne of the Majesty in the heavens in His ministry in the sanctuary and the true tabernacle, which the Lord pitched, and not man. "Whereof *the Holy Ghost* also *is a witness to us:* for after that he had said before, this is the covenant that I will make with them after those days, saith the Lord, I will put My laws into their hearts, and in their minds will I write them; and their sins and iniquities will I remember no more. Now where remission of these is, there is no more offering for sin." Heb. 10:15–18.

And this is the "new and living way" which Christ, through the flesh, "hath consecrated for us"—for all mankind; and by which every soul may enter into the holiest of all—the holiest of all places, the holiest of all experiences, the holiest of all relationships, the holiest of all living. This new and living way He "hath consecrated for us through the flesh;" that is, He, coming in the flesh, identifying Himself with mankind in the flesh, has, for us who are in this flesh, consecrated a way from where we are to where He now is, at the right hand of the throne of the Majesty in the heavens in the holiest of all.

In His coming in the flesh—having been made in all things like unto us, and having been tempted in all points like as we are—He has identified Himself with every human soul just where that soul is. And from the place where every human soul is, He has consecrated for that soul a new and living way through all the vicissitudes and experiences of a whole lifetime, and even through death and the tomb, into the holiest of all, at the right hand of God for evermore.

O that consecrated way! consecrated by His temptations and sufferings, by His prayers and tears, by His holy living and sacrificial dying, by His triumphant resurrection and glorious ascension, and by His triumphal entry into the holiest of all, at the right hand of the throne of the Majesty in the heavens!

And this "way" He has consecrated for *us*. He, having become one of us, has made this way *our* way; it belongs to us. He has endowed every soul with divine *right* to walk in this consecrated way; and by His having done it Himself in the flesh—in our flesh—He has made it possible, yea, He has given actual assurance, that every human soul *can* walk in that way, in all that that way is; and by it enter fully and freely into the holiest of all.

He, as one of us, in our human nature, weak as we, laden with the sins of the world, in our sinful flesh, in this world, a whole lifetime, lived a life "holy, harmless, undefiled, separate from sinners," and "was made" and ascended "higher than the heavens." And by this He has made and consecrated a way by which, *in Him,* every believer can in this world, and for a whole lifetime, live a life holy, harmless, undefiled, separate from sinners, and as a consequence be made with Him higher than the heavens.

Perfection, perfection of character, is the Christian goal—perfection attained in human flesh in this world. Christ attained it in human flesh in this world, and thus made and consecrated a way by which, *in Him,* every believer can attain it. He, having attained it, has become our great High Priest, by His priestly ministry in the true sanctuary to enable us to attain it.

Perfection is the Christian's goal; and the High Priesthood and ministry of Christ in the true sanctuary is the only way by which any soul can attain this true goal in this world. "Thy way, O God, is in the sanctuary." Ps. 77:13.

"Having therefore, brethren, boldness to enter into the holiest by the blood of Jesus, by a new and living way, which He hath consecrated for us, through the veil, that is to say, His flesh; and having an High Priest over the house of God; *let us draw near* with a *true heart* in *full assurance of faith,* having our hearts sprinkled from an evil conscience, and our bodies washed with pure water." And "let us hold fast the profession of our faith without wavering; for He is faithful that promised."

"For *ye* are *not come* unto the mount that might be touched, and that burned with fire, nor unto blackness, and darkness, and tempest, and the sound of a trumpet, and the voice of words; which voice they that heard entreated that the word should not be spoken to them any more. . . . But ye *are come* unto Mount Zion, and unto the city of the living God, the heavenly Jerusalem, and to an innumerable company of angels, to the general assembly and church of the *first-born,* which are written in heaven, and to God the Judge of all, and to the spirits of just men made perfect, and *to Jesus* the Mediator of the new covenant, and *to the blood of sprinkling, that speaketh better things* than that of Abel."

O, then, "see that ye refuse not Him that speaketh. For if they escaped not who refused Him that spake on earth, much more shall not we escape, if we turn away from Him that speaketh from heaven." Heb. 12:18–25.

CHAPTER XIII

The Transgression and Abomination of Desolation

SUCH is the sacrifice, the priesthood, and the ministry, of Christ in His ministry in the sanctuary and the true tabernacle, which the Lord pitched, and not man. Such is the statement *in the book of Hebrews* of the truth, the merit, and the efficacy of the sacrifice, the priesthood, the sanctuary, and the ministry of Christ.

But it is not alone in the book of Hebrews that this great truth is found. For though it is not so directly stated, nor so fully discussed in any other place as it is in the book of Hebrews, it is recognized throughout the whole of the New Testament as truly as the sanctuary and ministry of the Levitical priesthood is recognized throughout the Old Testament, though it be not so directly stated, nor so fully discussed in any other place as in Exodus and Leviticus.

In the last book of the New Testament, in the very first chapter, there is seen "one like unto the Son of Man," clothed in the raiment of the high priest. Also in the midst of the throne and of the cherubim and of the elders there was seen "a Lamb as it had been slain." There also was seen a golden altar, and one with a golden censer offering incense, which, with the prayers of the saints, ascended up before God. There was seen the seven lamps of fire burning before the throne. There was seen the temple of God in heaven; "the temple of the tabernacle of the testimony." There it is promised and declared that they who have part in the first resurrection and upon whom the second death hath no power "shall be priests of God and of Christ, and shall reign with Him a thousand years" in that priesthood. And when the first heaven and the first earth shall have passed away, and there shall be found no place for them; and the new heaven and the new earth shall have been brought in, with the holy city descending out of heaven from God, the tabernacle of God being with men, He dwelling with them, they His people, and God Himself with them, and their God; when He shall have wiped away all tears from their eyes, and there shall be no more death, neither sorrow nor crying, neither any more pain and the former things shall have passed away; then, and not until then, is it declared of the city of God: "I saw no temple therein."

Thus it is just as certain that there is a priesthood, a priestly ministry, and a sanctuary, in this dispensation, as that there was in the old: yes, even more truly; for though there was a sanctuary, a priesthood, and a ministry in the old dispensation, it was all only a figure for the time then present—a figure of this which now is the true, and which is in heaven.

This true priesthood, ministry, and sanctuary of Christ in heaven is too plain in the New Testament to be by any possibility denied. Yet, in the face of all this, it is a thing that is hardly ever thought of; it is a thing almost unknown, and even hardly believed, in the Christian world to-day.

Why is this, and how could it ever be? There is a cause. The Scripture tells it, and facts demonstrate it.

In the book of Daniel, seventh chapter, there was seen by the prophet, in vision, the four winds of heaven striving upon the great sea; "and four great beasts came up from the sea, diverse one from another. The first was like a lion, and had eagle's wings;" which symbolized the world-kingdom of Babylon. The second was like a bear, which raised itself up on one side, and had three ribs in the mouth of it; which symbolized the united world-kingdom of Media and Persia. The third was like a leopard, which had four heads and four wings of a fowl; which symbolized the world-dominion of Alexander the Great and Grecia. The fourth beast was "dreadful and terrible, and strong exceedingly; and it had great iron teeth: it devoured and brake in pieces, and stamped the residue with the feet of it: and it was diverse from all the beasts that were before it; and it had ten horns." This great beast symbolized the world-empire of Rome, diverse from all that were before it; because it was not originally a kingdom or monarchy, but a republic. The ten horns symbolized the ten kingdoms that were planted in the territory of Western Rome when that empire was annihilated.

Then says the prophet: "I considered the horns [the ten

horns], and, behold, there came up among them another little horn, before whom there were three of the first horns plucked up by the roots: and, behold, in this horn were eyes like the eyes of man, and a mouth speaking great things." The prophet beheld and considered this little horn, clear through until "the judgment was set, and the books were opened." And when this judgment was set and the books were opened, he says: "I beheld *then* [at that time] because of the voice of the great words which the horn spake: I beheld even till the beast was slain, and his body destroyed, and given to the burning flame."

Note the remarkable change in expression in this latter statement. The prophet beheld the little horn from the time of its rise clear through to the time when "the judgment was set, and the books were opened." *At that time* he beheld the little horn; and just now, *particularly* "because of the voice of the great words which the horn spake." And he continued to behold that same thing—that same little horn—until the end and till its destruction. But when its destruction comes, the word that describes it is not that the *little horn* was broken or destroyed, but that the "*beast* was slain, and *his* body destroyed, and given to the burning flame."

This shows that the little horn is but another phase of the original fourth, or dreadful and terrible, beast that the little horn is but the continuation of the dreadful and terrible beast, in its very disposition, spirit, and aims, only under a variant form. And as the fourth world power, the dreadful and terrible beast in its original form was Rome; so the little horn in its workings is but the continuation of Rome—of the spirit and working of Rome, under this form.

The explanation of this, given in the same chapter, confirms that which has been stated. For, of this little horn it is said that it is to be "diverse from the first;" that he "shall speak great words against the Most High, and shall wear out the saints of the Most High, and think to change times and laws" of the Most High. It is also said that the "same horn made war with the saints, and prevailed against them; until the Ancient of days came, and judgment was given to the saints of the Most High; and the time came that the saints possessed the kingdom." All these things are true, and this is the description, of latter Rome throughout.

And all this is confirmed by latter Rome herself. For Leo the Great was pope A.D. 440 to A.D. 461, in the very time when the former Rome was in its very last days, when it was falling rapidly to ruin. And Leo the Great declared in a sermon that the former Rome was but the promise of the latter Rome; that the glories of the former were to be reproduced in Catholic Rome; that Romulus and Remus were but the forerunners of Peter and Paul; that the successors of Romulus therefore were the precursors of the successors of Peter; and that, as the former Rome had ruled the world, so the latter Rome, by the see of the holy blessed Peter as head of the world, would dominate the earth. This conception of Leo's was never lost from the Papacy. And when, only fifteen years afterward, the Roman Empire had, as such, perished, and only the Papacy survived the ruin, and firmly held place and power in Rome, this conception of Leo's was only the more strongly, and with the more certitude, held and asserted.

That conception was also intentionally and systematically developed. The Scriptures were industriously studied and ingeniously perverted to maintain it. By a perverse application of the Levitical system of the Old Testament, the authority and eternity of the Roman priesthood had already been established.*

And now, by perverse deductions "from the New Testament, the authority and eternity of Rome herself was established."

Taking the ground that she is the only true continuation of original Rome, upon that the Papacy took the ground that wherever the New Testament cites, or refers to, the authority of original Rome, *she* is now meant, because she is the only true continuation of original Rome. Accordingly, where the New Testament enjoins submission to "the powers that be," or obedience to "governors," it means the Papacy; because the only power and the only governors that then were, were Roman, and the papal power was the true continuation of the Roman.

"Every passage was seized on where submission to the powers that be is enjoined; every instance cited where obedience had actually been rendered to the imperial officials; special emphasis being laid on the sanction which Christ Himself had given to Roman dominion by pacifying the world through Augustus, by

---

*"The *bishops* now [the latter part of the second century] wished to be thought to correspond with the *high priest* of the Jews; the *presbyters* were said to come in place of the *priests;* and the *deacons* were made parallel with the Levites.

"In like manner the comparison of the Christian *oblations* with the Jewish victims and sacrifices produced many unnecessary rites, and by decrees corrupted the very doctrine of the holy Supper; which was converted sooner, in fact, than one would think, into a *sacrifice.*"—*Mosheim's "Ecclesiastical History," Cen. II, part II, chap. II, par. 4; and chap. IV, par. 4.*

being born at the time of the taxing, by paying tribute to Cæsar, by saying to Pilate, 'Thou couldst have no power at all against Me except it were given thee from above.'"—*Bryce*. And since Christ had recognized the authority of Pilate, who was but the representative of Rome; who should dare to disregard the authority of the Papacy, the true continuation of that authority, to which even the Lord from heaven had submitted!

And it was only the logical culmination of this assumption when Pope Boniface VIII presented himself in the sight of the multitude, clothed in a cuirass, with a helmet on his head, and a sword in his hand held aloft, and proclaimed: "There is no other Cæsar, nor king, nor emperor than I, the Sovereign Pontiff and Successor of the Apostles;" and, when further he declared, *ex cathedra:* "We therefore assert, define, and pronounce that it is necessary to salvation to believe that every human being is subject to the Pontiff of Rome."

This is proof enough that the little horn of the seventh chapter of Daniel is Papal Rome, and that it is in spirit and purpose intentionally the continuation of original Rome.

Now, in the eighth chapter of Daniel, this subject is taken up again. First, there is seen by the prophet in vision a ram, with two horns which were high, but one higher than the other, corresponding to the bear lifting itself up on one side higher than the other. This is declared plainly by the angel to mean "the kings of Media and Persia." Next the prophet saw "an he goat" coming from the west on the face of the whole earth, touching not the ground, and he had a notable horn between his eyes. He overthrew the ram, brake his two horns, cast him down to the ground, and stamped upon him; and there was none that could deliver the ram out of his hand. This is declared by the angel to mean "the king of Grecia: and the great horn that is between his eyes is the first king." The he-goat waxed very great, and when he was strong, the notable horn was broken, and in place of it there came up four notable ones toward the four winds of heaven. This is declared by the angel to mean that "four kingdoms shall stand up out of the nation, but not in his [Alexander's] power."

Out of one of these divisions of the empire of Alexander, the prophet next saw that there "came forth a *little horn*, which waxed exceeding great, toward the south, and toward the east, and toward the pleasant land." The directions named show that this power rose and waxed exceeding great from *the west*. This is explained by the angel to mean, "in the latter time of their kingdom [the four divisions of Grecia], when the transgressors are come to the full, a king of fierce countenance, and understanding dark sentences, shall stand up." "And it waxed great, even to the host of heaven; and it cast down some of the host and of the stars to the ground, and stamped upon them." "And his power shall be mighty, but not by his own power: and he shall destroy wonderfully, and shall prosper, and practice, and shall destroy the mighty and the holy people. And through his policy also he shall cause craft to prosper in his hand; and he shall magnify himself in his heart, and by peace shall destroy many: he shall also stand up against the Prince of princes ["He magnified himself even to the prince of the host." Verse 11]; but he shall be broken without hand."

These specifications show that the little horn of the eighth chapter of Daniel represents Rome from the time of its rise, at the destruction of the Grecian Empire, to the end of the world, when it is "broken *without hand*," by that stone "cut out of the mountain *without hands*," which then breaks in pieces and consumes all earthly kingdoms. Dan. 2:34, 35, 44, 45.

We have seen that in the seventh chapter of Daniel the little horn, though *as such* representing only the latter phase of Rome, yet does really represent Rome in both its phases—Rome from beginning to end; because when the time comes that the *"little horn"* is to be broken and destroyed, it is indeed *"the beast"* that is "slain, and *his* body destroyed, and given to the burning flame." Thus the thought with which the story of the little horn closes in Daniel 7 is continued in Daniel 8, with reference to the same power. In Daniel 8 the expression "little horn" covers the whole of Rome in *both its phases*, just as is shown in the closing expressions concerning the "little horn" in Daniel 7; as is shown also by the expressions "the abomination of desolation" and "the transgression of desolation," being applied to Rome in both its phases (Dan. 9:26, 27; Matt. 24:15; Dan. 11:31; 12:11; 8:11, 13); and as is confirmed by the teaching and history of latter Rome itself. It is all one, except only that all that is stated of the former Rome is true and *intensified* in the latter Rome.

And now let us consider further the scripture expressions in Daniel 8 concerning this little horn power. In verses 11 and 25, of this little horn power it is said: "He shall magnify himself in his heart." "He magnified himself even to [or against] the prince of

the host;" and "he shall also stand up against [or reign in opposi-
tion to] the Prince of princes." This is explained in 2 Thessalonians, second chapter, where the apostle, in correcting wrong
impressions which the Thessalonians had received concerning
the immediate coming of the Lord, says: "Let no man deceive
you by any means: for that day shall not come, except there come
a falling away first, and that man of sin be revealed, the son of
perdition; who *opposeth* and *exalteth himself* above *all that is called
God, or that is worshiped;* so that he as God sitteth in the temple of
God, showing himself that he is God. Remember ye not, that,
when I was yet with you, I told you these things?" 2 Thess. 2:3–5.

Plainly this scripture describes the same power that is represented by the little horn in Daniel 8. But there are other consid-
erations which more fully show it. He says that when he was at
Thessalonica with the brethren he had *told* them these very
things, which now he *writes.* In Acts 17:1–3, is the record concerning Paul when he was yet with the Thessalonians, as follows:
"Now when they had passed through Amphipolis and Apollonia,
they came to Thessalonica, where was a synagogue of the Jews:
and Paul, as his manner was, went in unto them, and three
Sabbath days reasoned with them out of the Scriptures." And in
this reasoning with them out of the Scriptures, he told them
about this falling away which should come, in which would be the
revealing of the man of sin, the mystery of iniquity, the son of
perdition, who would oppose himself to God, and would exalt
himself above all that is called God or that is worshiped, even
putting himself in the place of God, and passing himself off for
God.

In reasoning with the people out of the Scriptures, where in
the Scriptures did Paul find the revelation from which he could
tell to the Thessalonians all this? It was in this eighth chapter of
Daniel where the apostle found it; and from this it was that he
told it to them while he was there. For in the eighth chapter of
Daniel are the very expressions which he uses in 2 Thessalonians,
of which he says, "Remember ye not, that, when I was yet with
you, I told you these things?" This fixes the time to be *after the
apostles' days,* when Rome magnified itself "even to the Prince of
the host" and "against the Prince of princes;" and connects it
directly with the falling away, or apostasy, which developed the
Papacy, or Rome, in its latter and ultimate phase.

Now let us read verses 11 and 12 of Daniel 8, and it will be plainly seen that here is exactly the place where Paul found the scripture from which he taught the Thessalonians concerning the "man of sin" and the "mystery of iniquity:" "Yea, he magnified himself even to the Prince of the host, and by him the daily sacrifice was taken away, and *the place of his sanctuary was cast down.* And an host was given him against the daily sacrifice by reason of transgression, and it cast down the truth to the ground; and it practiced and prospered."

This plainly points out that which took away the priesthood, the ministry, and the sanctuary of God, and of Christianity.

Let us read it again. "Yea, he [the little horn—the man of sin] magnified himself even to the Prince of the host ["against the Prince of princes"—Christ], and by him [the man of sin] the daily sacrifice [the continual service, the ministry, and the priesthood of Christ] was taken away, and the place of His sanctuary [the sanctuary of the prince of the host, of the Prince of princes—Christ] was cast down. And an host was given him [the man of sin] against the daily sacrifice [against the continual service, of the ministry of Christ, the Prince of the host] by reason of transgression, and it cast down the truth to the ground; and it practiced, and prospered."

It was "by reason of transgression," that is, by reason of sin, that this power gained "the host" that was used to cast down the truth to the ground, to shut away from the church and the world Christ's priesthood, His ministry, and His sanctuary; and to cast it all down to the ground and tread it underfoot. It was by reason of transgression that this was accomplished. Transgression is sin, and this is the consideration and the revelation upon which the apostle in 2 Thessalonians defines this power as the "man of sin" and the "mystery of iniquity."

In Daniel 8:11–13; 11:31; and 12:11, it will be noticed that the word *"sacrifice"* is in every case supplied. And it is wholly supplied; for in its place in the original there is no word at all. In the original the only word that stands in this place, is the word *tamid,* that is here translated *"daily,"* and in these places the expression "daily" does not refer to the daily *sacrifice* any more than it refers to the whole daily ministry or continual service of the sanctuary, of which the *sacrifice* was only a part. The word *tamid* in itself signifies "continuous or continual," "constant," "stable," "sure," "constantly," "evermore." Only such words as these express the thought of the original word, which in the text under consideration, is translated *"daily."* In Numbers 28 and 29 alone, the word is used seventeen times, referring to the *continual service in the sanctuary.*

And it is this continual service of Christ, the true High Priest, "who *continueth ever,"* and "who is consecrated *forevermore"* in "an unchangeable priesthood"—it is *this continual service* of our great High Priest, which the man of sin, the Papacy, *has taken away.* It is the sanctuary and the true tabernacle in which this true High Priest exercises His *continual ministry* that has been cast down by "the transgression of desolation." It is this ministry and this sanctuary that the "man of sin" has taken away from the church and shut away from the world, and has cast down to the ground and stamped upon; and in place of which it has set up itself "the abomination that maketh desolate." What the former Rome did physically to the visible or earthly sanctuary, which was "the figure of the true" (Dan. 9:26, 27; Matt. 24:15), that the latter Rome has done spiritually to the invisible or heavenly sanctuary that is itself the true." Dan. 11:31; 12:11; 8:11, 13.

In the foot-note quotation on page 67 it is shown that in the apostasy, the bishops, presbyters, deacons, and the eucharist, were made to succeed the high priest, priests, Levites and sacrifices of the Levitical system. Now by every evidence of the Scriptures, it is certain that, *in the order of God,* it was Christ and His ministry and sanctuary in heaven, and this alone, that in truth was the object of the Levitical system, and that is truly the Christian succession to that system. Therefore when in and by the apostasy the system of bishops as high priests, presbyters as priests, deacons as Levites, and the Supper as sacrifice, was insinuated as the Christian succession to the Levitical system, this of itself was nothing else than to put this false system of the apostasy in the place of the true, completely to shut out the true, and, finally, to cast it down to the ground and stamp upon it.

And this is how it is that this great Christian truth of the true priesthood, ministry, and sanctuary of Christ is not known to the Christian world to-day. The "man of sin" has taken it away, and cast it down to the ground, and stamped upon it. The "mystery of iniquity" has hid this great truth from the church and the world during all these ages, in which the man of sin has held place in the world, and has passed itself off as God, and its iniquitous host as the church of God.

And yet, even the "man of sin," the "mystery of iniquity," itself bears witness to the necessity of such a service in the church in behalf of sins. For though the "man of sin," the "mystery of iniquity," has taken away the true priesthood, ministry, and sanctuary of Christ, and has cast these down to the ground to be stamped upon, and has completely hid them from the eyes of the Christian world; yet she did not utterly throw away the *idea.* No, she threw away *the true,* and cast down *the true* to the ground; but, *retaining the idea,* in the place of the true she built up in her own realm an utterly false structure.

In the place of Christ, the true and divine High Priest of God's own appointment in heaven, she has substituted a human, sinful, and sinning priesthood on earth. In the place of the *continual,* heavenly ministry of Christ in His true priesthood upon His true sacrifice, she has substituted only an *interval* ministry of a human, earthly, sinful, and sinning priesthood in the once-a-day "daily sacrifice of the mass." And in the place of the sanctuary and the true tabernacle, which the Lord pitched, and not man, she has substituted her own meeting-places of wood and stone, to which she applies the term "sanctuary." Thus, instead of the one continual High Priest, the one continual ministry, and the one continual sanctuary in heaven, which God has ordained, and which is the only true, she has devised out of her own heart and substituted for the only true, many high priests, many ministries, many sacrifices, and many sanctuaries, *on earth,* which in every possible relation are only human and utterly false.

And *it can never take away sin.* No earthly priesthood, no earthly ministry, no earthly sacrifice, or service, in any earthly sanctuary, can ever take away sin. In the book of Hebrews we have seen that even the priesthood, the ministry, the sacrifice, and the service in the earthly sanctuary—the very service which the Lord Himself ordained on earth—never took away sin. The inspired record is that they never *did* take away sin, and that they never *could* take away sin.

It is only the priesthood and the ministry of Christ that can ever take away sin. And this is a priesthood and a ministry *in heaven,* and of a sanctuary that is *in heaven.* For when Christ was on earth He was not a priest, and if He had remained on earth until this hour, He would not yet be a priest; as it stands written, "If He were on earth, He should not be a priest." Heb. 8:4. Thus, by plain word and abundant illustration, God has demonstrated that no earthly priesthood, sacrifice, or ministry can ever take away sin.

If any such could take away sin, then why could not that which

God Himself ordained on earth take away sin? If any such could take away sin, then why change the priesthood and the ministry from earth to heaven? Therefore, by the plain word of the Lord, it is plain that the priesthood, the ministry, the sacrifice, and the sanctuary which the Papacy has set up and operates on earth can never take away sin; but, instead, only perpetuates sin, is a fraud, an imposture, and the very "transgression" and "abomination of desolation" is the most holy place.

And that this conclusion and statement as to what the papal system really is, is not extravagant nor far-fetched, is confirmed by the words of Cardinal Baronius, the standard annalist of the papacy. Writing of the tenth century, he says: "In this century *the abomination of desolation was seen in the temple of the Lord;* and in the See of St. Peter, reverenced by angels, were placed the most wicked of men; not pontiffs, but monsters." And the council of Rheims, in 991, declared the papacy to be "the man of sin, the mystery of iniquity."

CHAPTER XIV

The Time of Finishing the Mystery of God

BUT that imposture is not to last forever; thank the Lord! This great truth of the priesthood, ministry, and sanctuary of Christianity is not to be hid forever from the eyes of the church and the world. The mystery of iniquity arose, and so hid from the world the mystery of God that all the world followed it wondering. Rev. 13:3, 4. But the day comes when the mystery of iniquity shall be exposed, and the mystery of God in its own truth and purity shall shine forth once more; never more to be hid, but to accomplish its great purpose and be completely finished. For it is written that "in the days of the voice of the seventh angel, when he shall begin to sound, the mystery of God should be finished, as He hath declared to His servants the prophets." Rev. 10:7.

In the days of Christ and His apostles, the mystery of God was revealed in a fulness never before known, and was preached "to all nations for the obedience of faith." Rom. 16:25, 26. From the beginning of the world unto that time this mystery had "been hid in God;" had "been hid from ages and from generations," but was then "made manifest to His saints;" to whom "God would make known what is the riches of the glory of this mystery among the Gentiles; which is Christ is you, the hope of glory: whom we preach, warning every man, and teaching every man in all wisdom; that we may present every man perfect in Christ Jesus." Col. 1:26–29; Eph. 3:3, 5, 9.

But even at that same time, in the very days of the apostles, the "mystery of iniquity" did "already work." And it continued to work until it gained world-power and supremacy, and even power over the saints, the times, and the law of the Most High— standing up against the Prince of princes, magnifying itself even to the Prince of the host, putting itself in the place of worship of God, and passing itself off for God. And thus, again, but *not* this time *in God,* the mystery of God was "hid from ages and from generations." But *now,* again, in the days of the voice of the seventh angel, *even now,* the mystery of God which hath again been hid from ages and generations, *is made manifest to His saints* to whom *now* "God would make known what is the riches of the glory of this mystery among the Gentiles; which is Christ in you, the hope of glory: whom we preach, warning every man, and teaching every man in all wisdom; that we may present every man *perfect* in Christ Jesus."

And this, as we have already quoted, is itself according "as He hath declared to His servants the prophets." It is not alone the prophet of Patmos who declared that in this time, even now in our day, "the mystery of God should be finished." For when the angel of God made this proclamation in the vision of the prophet of Patmos, he had already, and long before, declared the same thing to His servants the prophets. And this proclamation on Patmos was only the declaration of the angel that that which God had long before declared to His servants the prophets should now surely be accomplished; and that with no more delay. The full proclamation of the angel is this: "And the angel which I saw stand upon the sea and upon the earth lifted up his hand to heaven, and sware by Him that liveth forever and ever, who created heaven, and the things that therein are, and the earth, and the things that therein are, and the sea, and the things which are therein, that there should be time ["delay," R. V] no longer: but in the days of the voice of the seventh angel, when he shall begin to sound, the mystery of God should be finished, as He hath declared to His servants the prophets." Rev. 10:5–7.

The one prophet to whom this thing was more fully and more plainly declared than to any other was the prophet Daniel. For not only did Daniel see the rise of this little horn, and see it magnify itself "even to the Prince of the host," and "stand up against the Prince of princes," and cast down to the ground His truth and His sanctuary and stamp upon them; but he also, *and in the same vision,* saw the truth and the sanctuary of Christ *delivered* from this little horn power, *rescued* from its blasphemous stamping, *lifted up* from the earth, and *exalted* to the heaven where it belongs. And it was in this part of the transactions in the vision that the heavenly ones seemed to be most interested; for, says Daniel: "Then I heard one saint speaking, and another saint said unto that certain saint ["the Wonderful Numberer"] which spake, How long shall be the vision concerning the daily sacrifice [the continual service], and the transgression of desolation, to give both the sanctuary and the host to be trodden underfoot? And He ["the Wonderful Numberer"] said unto me, Unto two thousand and three hundred days; *then* shall *the sanctuary be cleansed.*" Dan. 8:13, 14.

Then the angel Gabriel was commanded to make Daniel understand the vision. He began to do so, but when in the explanation he had reached the point concerning the many days of this vision, the astonishing and terrible things revealed in the vision overcame the prophet, and says he: "I Daniel fainted, and was sick certain days; afterward I rose up, and did the king's business; and I was astonished at the vision, but none understood it." Dan. 8:27. So far as the explanation had proceeded, it was easily understood: for it was plainly spoken that the ram represented the kings of Media and Persia; and the rough goat the king of Grecia; and, in view of the explanation that had already been made in the second and seventh chapters of Daniel, the description of the next great power after Grecia was easily understood so far as the angel could then go with the explanation. But in the very midst of the explanation of the most important part of it, Daniel fainted: and so the most material and essential part of the explanation was missed, and "none understood it."

However, the prophet sought diligently for an understanding of the vision. And after the destruction of Babylon, in the first year of the king of the Medes and Persians the angel Gabriel came to Daniel again, and said: "O Daniel, I am now come forth to give thee skill and understanding." Dan. 9:1, 22. And it was understanding in this particular vision which he was explaining when Daniel fainted, that he now came to give. Accordingly he directs Daniel's attention first of all to that vision: for he said: "At the beginning of thy supplications the commandment came forth, and I am come to shew thee; for thou art greatly beloved: therefore understand the matter, and *consider the vision.*" Verse 23. Having thus directed the prophet's attention to the vision, the angel begins immediately to discuss the *time* mentioned in the vision—the very part of the vision which, because of Daniel's fainting, had been left unexplained. Thus he says: "Seventy weeks are determined upon thy people and upon thy holy city." Verse 24.

The word *"determined"* signifies "limited," "restricted within bounds," "to mark off and fix the bounds." In explaining the vision at the first, the angel had come to the point of the time—the "many days," the "two thousand and three hundred days" of the vision. Now, as he tells Daniel to consider the vision, he begins immediately to speak concerning these days and to explain the events of them. "Seventy weeks," or four hundred and ninety of these days, are limited and restricted to the Jews and Jerusalem: and this also marks the limitation of the Jews and Jerusalem as God's special people and city. For these are prophetic days, in which each day is a year: the seventy weeks, or the four hundred and ninety days, thus making four hundred and ninety *years* of the two thousand and three hundred days which are two thousand and three hundred years. The beginning of the four hundred and ninety years is thus also the beginning of the two thousand and three hundred years.

The story of the "seventy weeks," or four hundred and ninety years, is given by the angel as follows: "Know therefore and understand, that from the going forth of the commandment to restore and to build Jerusalem unto the Messiah the Prince shall be seven weeks, and threescore and two weeks: the street shall be built again, and the wall, even in troublous times. And *after threescore and two weeks* shall *Messiah be cut off,* but not for himself: and the people of the prince that shall come shall *destroy* the city and *the sanctuary;* and the end thereof shall be with a flood, and unto the end of the war desolations are determined. And He shall confirm the covenant with many for one week: and in the midst of the week He shall cause the sacrifices and oblation to cease," and "upon the wing of abominations shall come one that maketh desolate, ["and upon the battlements shall be the idols of the desolator."—*A. V. margin*] even until the consummation, and that determined shall be poured upon the desolator." Dan. 9:25–27; 9:27, R. V.; 9:27, margin.

The commandment to restore and to build Jerusalem here referred to went forth in the year 457 B.C., and is recorded in the seventh chapter of Ezra. The decree was issued from Babylon, and was addressed, *first,* to Ezra, empowering him to leave Babylon and to take with him such people and materials as were supplied for the work of restoring Jerusalem, and the worship of God therein; and, *secondly,* "to all the treasurers which are beyond the river" Euphrates, directing them to supply whatever was required by Ezra for the carrying on of the work. It was the fifth month of the year when Ezra reached Jerusalem, so that about half the year 457 B.C. was gone, which would give about the year 456½ as the time of the beginning of the four hundred and ninety years and the two thousand and three hundred years.

From that time four hundred and eighty-three years were to reach "to the Messiah the Prince," which would reach twenty-six and one-half years into the Christian era, or into the year A.D. 27; which is *the very year* of Christ's appearance as the Messiah in His public ministry, when He was baptized in Jordan and anointed with the Holy Ghost. Mark 7:9–11; Matt. 3:13–17. After this He, the Messiah, was to "confirm the covenant" "for one week"—the remaining week of the seventy. But in the midst of that week He would "cause the sacrifice and the oblation to cease" by the sacrifice of Himself on the cross. In the midst of the week would be at the end of three and a half of the seven years from the fall of A.D. 27. This gives the date the spring A.D. 31, *the very time when the Saviour was crucified,* and thus by the sacrifice of Himself—the only sacrifice for sins—forever caused the sacrifice and the oblation to cease. Then the veil of the earthly temple "was rent in twain from the top to the bottom," showing that the service of God there was ended, and the earthly house was desolate.

There was yet the last half of the seventieth week remaining as the limit of the time of special favor to the Jews and Jerusalem. This half of the week, beginning in the spring of A.D. 31, extended to the fall of A.D. 34. In that time "they which were scattered abroad upon the persecution that arose about Stephen ["went everywhere preaching the word"] traveled as far as Phenice, and Cyprus, and Antioch, preaching the word to *none but unto the Jews only.*" Acts 11:19; 8:4. But when this time was expired, and the Jews had confirmed themselves in the rejection of the Messiah and His gospel, then was their decision accepted; and under the leadership of both Peter and Paul the door of faith was opened fully to the Gentiles; *to whom pertains the remaining portion of the two thousand and three hundred years.*

After the four hundred and ninety years of the limitation upon the Jew and Jerusalem, there yet remained one thousand eight hundred and ten years to the Gentiles. This period, beginning, as we have found, in the fall of A.D. 34, reaches inevitably to the fall of A.D. 1844, and marks *that* date as the expiration of the two thousand and three hundred years. *And at that time,* upon the word of the "Wonderful Numberer" in Daniel 8:14, *"then shall the sanctuary be cleansed.*" In 1844 also was the very time of "the days of the voice of the seventh angel, when he shall begin to sound," and when "the mystery of God should be finished, as He hath declared to His servants the prophets."

At that time there would be broken up the horror of great darkness by which the mystery of iniquity had hid from ages and generations the mystery of God. At that time the sanctuary and the true tabernacle, and the truth of it, would be lifted up from the ground where the man of sin had cast them down and stamped upon them, and would be exalted to the heaven where they belong, and whence they will shine forth in such light as that the earth shall be lightened with the glory. At that time the transcendent truth of the priesthood and ministry of Christ would be rescued from the oblivion to which the abomination and transgression of desolation had consigned it, and would once more and forever stand in its true and heavenly place in the faith of the church, accomplishing in every true believer that perfection which is the eternal purpose of God which He purposed in Christ Jesus our Lord.

CHAPTER XV

The Cleansing of the Sanctuary

THE cleansing of the sanctuary and the finishing of the mystery of God are identical as to time; and are also so closely related as to be practically identical in character and event.

In the "figure of the true" in the sanctuary service made visible, the round of service was completed annually; and the *cleansing of the sanctuary* was the *finishing* of that figurative and annual service. And this cleansing of the sanctuary was the taking out of and away from the sanctuary all "the uncleanness of the children of Israel" "because of their transgressions in all their sins," which, by the ministry of the priesthood in the sanctuary had been brought into the sanctuary during the service of the year.

The finishing of this work of the sanctuary and for the sanctuary was, likewise, the finishing of the work *for the people.* For in that day of the cleansing of the sanctuary, which was the day of atonement, whosoever of the people did not by searching of heart, confession, and putting away of sin, take part in the service of the cleansing of the sanctuary was cut off forever. Thus the cleansing of the sanctuary extended to *the people,* and included *the people,* as truly as it did the sanctuary itself. And whosoever of the people was not included in the cleansing of the sanctuary, and was not *himself cleansed,* equally with the sanctuary, from all iniquity and transgression and sin, was cut off forever. Lev. 16:15–19; 29–34; 23:27–32.

And this was all "a figure for the time then present." That sanctuary, sacrifice, priesthood, and ministry was a figure of *the true,* which is the sanctuary, sacrifice, priesthood, and ministry of Christ. And that *cleansing* of the sanctuary was a figure of the true, which is the cleansing of the sanctuary and the true tabernacle which the Lord pitched and not man, from all the uncleanness of the believers in Jesus because of all their transgressions in all their sins. And the *time* of this cleansing of the true is declared in the words of the Wonderful Numberer to be "unto two thousand and three hundred days, then shall the sanctuary be cleansed:" which is the sanctuary of Christ in A.D. 1844.

And, indeed, the sanctuary of which Christ is the High Priest is the only one that could possibly be cleansed in 1844; because it is the only one that there is. The sanctuary that was a figure for the time then present was destroyed by the army of the Romans who came and destroyed that city (Dan. 9:26) and that sanctuary; and even its place was to be desolate "even until the consummation." Therefore the only sanctuary that could possibly be cleansed at the time referred to by the Wonderful Numberer, at the end of the two thousand and three hundred days, was alone the sanctuary of Christ—the sanctuary of which Christ is High Priest and Minister; the sanctuary and the true tabernacle of which Christ, at the right hand of God, is true Priest and Minister; the sanctuary and true tabernacle "which the Lord pitched, and not man."

What this cleansing means is plainly declared in the very scripture which we are now studying,—Dan. 9:24–28. For the angel of God, in telling to Daniel the truth concerning the two thousand and three hundred days, tells also the great object of the Lord in this time as it relates to both the Jews and the Gentiles. The seventy weeks, or four hundred and ninety years, of the limitation upon the Jews and Jerusalem is definitely declared to be "to *finish the transgression,* and to *make an end of sins,* and to *make reconciliation for iniquity,* and to *bring in everlasting righteousness,* and to *seal up the vision and prophecy,* and to *anoint the most Holy.*" Daniel 9:24.

That is the true purpose of God in the sanctuary and its service in all time: whether in the figure or in the true; whether for Jews or for Gentiles; whether on earth or in heaven. Seventy weeks, or four hundred and ninety years, was the limitation set for the Jews to have this accomplished for and in themselves. To accomplish this, to that people, of all people, Christ Himself came in person to show to them the Way, and to lead them in this Way. But they would not have it. Instead of seeing in Him the gracious One who would finish transgression, and make an end of sins, and make reconciliation for iniquity, and bring in everlasting righteousness, to every soul, they saw in Him only "Beelzebub the prince of the devils;" only one instead of whom they would readily choose a murderer; only one who as King they would openly repudiate, and choose a Roman Cæsar as their only king; only one whom they counted as fit only to be crucified out of the world. For such a people as that, and in such a people as that, could He finish transgression, and make an end of sins, and make reconciliation for iniquity, and bring in everlasting righteousness?—Impossible: impossible by their own persistent rebellion. Instead of His being allowed by them to do such a gracious and wonderful work for them, from the depths of divine pity and sorrow He was compelled to say *to* them: "O Jerusalem, Jerusalem, thou that killest the prophets, and stonest them which are sent unto thee, how often would I have gathered thy children together, even as a hen gathereth her chickens under her wings, and ye would not! Behold, your house is left unto you desolate." "The kingdom of God shall be taken from you, and given to a nation bringing forth the fruits thereof." Matt. 23:37, 38; 21:43.

The nation to whom the kingdom of God was given, upon its rejection by the Jews, was the Gentiles. And that which was to be done for the Jews in the four hundred and ninety years which were limited to them, but which they would not at all allow to be done for them—*that* is the identical thing to be done for the Gentiles, to whom the kingdom of God is given, in the eighteen hundred and ten years allotted to them. And that work is "to finish the transgression, and to make an end of sins, and to make reconciliation for iniquity, and to bring in everlasting righteousness, and to seal up the vision and prophecy, and to anoint the most Holy." This can be done alone in the finishing of the mystery of God in the cleansing of the true Christian sanctuary. And this is done in the cleansing of the true sanctuary, only in the finishing of transgression and making an end of sins in the *perfecting* of the believers in Jesus, on the one hand; and on the other hand in the finishing of transgression and making an end of sins in *the destruction of the wicked* and the cleansing of the universe from all taint of sin that has ever been upon it.

The finishing of the mystery of God is the ending of the work of the gospel. And the ending of the work of the gospel is, *first, the taking away of all vestige of sin* and the bringing in of everlasting righteousness—Christ fully formed—within each believer, God alone manifest in the flesh of each believer in Jesus; and, *secondly,* on the other hand, the work of the gospel being finished means only the destruction of all who then shall not have received the gospel (2 Thess. 1:7–10): for it is not the way of the Lord to continue men in life when the only possible use they will make of life is to heap up more misery for themselves.

Again, in the service of the earthly sanctuary, we have seen that when the work of the gospel in the annual course was finished in behalf of those who had taken part in it, then all those who had taken no part in it were cut *off.* "Which was a figure for the time then present," and which plainly teaches that in the service of the true sanctuary when the work of the gospel shall have been finished for all those who have a part in it, then all those who do not have a part in it will be cut off. Thus, in both respects, the finishing of the mystery of God is the final ending of sin.

The service in the earthly sanctuary shows also that in order for the sanctuary to be cleansed and the course of the gospel service there to be finished, it must first be finished *in the people* who have a part in the service. That is to say: In the sanctuary itself, transgression could not be finished, an end of sins and reconciliation for iniquity could not be made, and everlasting righteousness could not be brought in, until all this had been accomplished *in each person* who had a part in the service of the sanctuary. The sanctuary itself could not be cleansed until each of the worshipers had been cleansed. The sanctuary itself could not be cleansed so long as, *by the confessions of the people and the intercessions of the priests,* there was pouring into the sanctuary a stream of iniquities, transgressions, and sins. The cleansing of the sanctuary, *as to the sanctuary itself,* was the taking out of and away from the sanctuary all the transgressions of the people which, by the service of the priests, had been taken into the sanctuary during the service of the year. And this stream must be stopped at its fountain in the hearts and lives of the worshipers, before the sanctuary itself could possibly be cleansed.

Therefore the very first work in the cleansing of the sanctuary was the cleansing of the people. That which was preliminary and essential to the cleansing of the sanctuary itself, to the finishing of transgression and bringing in everlasting righteousness, there, was the finishing of transgression, and the making an end of sins, and making reconciliation for iniquity and bringing in everlasting righteousness *in the heart and life of each one of the people* themselves. When the stream that flowed into the sanctuary was thus stopped at its source, then, and then alone, could the sanctuary itself be cleansed from the sins and transgressions which, *from the people, by the intercession of the priests,* had flowed into the sanctuary.

And all that "was a figure for the time then present"—a "figure of the true." Therefore by this we are plainly taught that the service of our great High Priest in the cleansing of the true sanctuary must be preceded by the cleansing of each one of the believers, the cleansing of each one who has a part in that service of the true High Priest in the true sanctuary. It is plain that transgression must be finished, an end of sins and reconciliation for all iniquity must be made, and everlasting righteousness must be brought in, in the heart's experience of every believer in Jesus, before the cleansing of the true sanctuary can be accomplished.

And this is the very object of the true priesthood in the true sanctuary. The sacrifices, the priesthood, and the ministry in the sanctuary which was but a figure for the time then present, could not really take away sin, could not make the comers thereunto perfect. Whereas the sacrifice, the priesthood, and the ministry of Christ in the true sanctuary does take away sins forever, does make the comers thereunto *perfect,* does *perfect "forever* them that are sanctified."

CHAPTER XVI

The Times of Refreshing

AND *now*, in this time of the consummation of the hope of all the ages, in this time when the true sanctuary is truly to be cleansed, in this time when the work of the gospel is to be completed and the mystery of God indeed finished—*now* is the time of all the times that ever were in the world, when the believers in Jesus—the blessed objects of His glorious priesthood and wondrous intercessions in the true sanctuary—shall be partakers of the full measure of His heavenly grace; and shall have in their lives transgression finished, an end of sins and reconciliation for iniquity made forevermore, and, in the perfection of truth, everlasting righteousness brought in.

This is precisely and alone the purpose of the priesthood and ministry of Christ in the true sanctuary. Is not that priesthood sufficient? Is not His ministry effectual to accomplish its purpose?—Most assuredly. Only by that means can it be possible for this thing ever to be accomplished. No soul can ever himself finish transgression, or make an end of sins, or make reconciliation for iniquity, or bring in everlasting righteousness, in his own life. For that ever to be done, it must be done *alone* by the priesthood and ministry of Him who gave Himself, and who was given, that He might accomplish this very thing for every soul, and present every soul "holy and unblameable and unreprovable" in the sight of God.

Every one whose heart is inclined to truth and right desires that this thing shall be done. Only the priesthood and ministry of Christ can do it. Now is the time of the complete and effectual doing of it for evermore. Then let us believe in Him who is doing this, and trust Him in the doing of it, that He does it completely and forevermore.

This is the time, and this is the work, of which it is written, that "there should be delay no longer." And why *should* there be delay any longer? When the priesthood of our great High Priest is efficient, and when His sacrifice and ministry are all sufficient, in that which is promised and in that for which every believer hopes, then why should there be delay any longer in the finishing of transgression, the making an end of sin, the making of reconciliation for iniquity, and the bringing in of everlasting righteousness, to each believing soul? Then let us trust Him to do that which He has given Himself to do, and which *He alone* can possibly do. Let us trust Him in this, and receive in its fullness all that belongs to every soul who believes in and implicitly trusts the Apostle and High Priest of our profession—Christ Jesus.

We have seen that the little horn—the man of sin, the mystery of iniquity—has put his own earthly, human, and sinful priesthood, ministry, and sanctuary in the place of the heavenly and holy priesthood, ministry, and sanctuary. In this priesthood and service of the mystery of iniquity, the sinner confesses his sins to the priest, and *goes on sinning*. Indeed, in that priesthood and ministry there is no power to do anything else than to go on sinning; even after they have confessed their sins. But, sad as the question may be, is it not too true that those who are not of the mystery of iniquity, but who really believe in Jesus and in His priesthood and ministry—is it not too true that even these also confess their sins, and *then go on sinning?*

But is this fair to our great High Priest, to His sacrifice, and to His blessed ministry? Is it fair that we should thus put Him, His sacrifice, and His ministry, practically upon a level with that of the "abomination of desolation," and to say that in Him and in His ministry there is no more power or virtue than there is in that of the "mystery of iniquity"? May the Lord forever save His church and people this day, with no more delay, from thus bringing down so low our great High Priest, His awful sacrifice, and His glorious ministry.

Let our trust in our great High Priest be true, and let it be truly implicit. By Protestants there is often remark made of the blind unwisdom of Catholics in their so fully trusting to the priest. And, with respect to any earthly priesthood, the thought is correct. And yet implicit trust of the priest is eternally right: but it must be trust of the *right Priest*. Such trust in a false priesthood is most ruinous; but *the principle* of implicit trust in the Priest is eternally right. And Jesus Christ is the right Priest. Therefore every one who believes in Jesus Christ, in the sacrifice which He has made, in the priesthood and ministry which He exercises in the true sanctuary, must not only confess his sins, but he must then forever implicitly trust that true High Priest in His ministry in the true sanctuary to *finish* transgression, to *make an end* of sins, to make *reconciliation* for iniquity, and to bring in *everlasting righteousness,* in his heart and life.

Everlasting righteousness, remember. Not a righteousness for to-day and sin to-morrow, and righteousness again and sin again. *That* is not everlasting righteousness. Everlasting righteousness is righteousness that is brought in and stays everlastingly in the life of him who has believed and confessed, and who *still further believes* and *receives* this everlasting righteousness in the place of all sin and all sinning. This alone is everlasting righteousness; this alone is eternal redemption from sin. And this unspeakable blessing is the gracious gift of God by the heavenly ministry which He has established in our behalf in the priesthood and ministry of Christ in the heavenly sanctuary.

Accordingly, to-day, just now, "while it is called to-day," as never before, the word of God to all people is, "Repent ye therefore, and be converted, that your sins may be blotted out, when the times of refreshing shall come ["that so there may come seasons of refreshing," R. V.] from the presence of the Lord; and He shall send Jesus Christ, which before was preached unto you: whom the heaven must receive until the time of restitution of all things." Acts 3:19–21.

The time of the coming of the Lord and the restitution of all things is indeed at the very doors. And when Jesus comes, it is to take His people unto Himself. It is to present to Himself His glorious church, "not having spot, or wrinkle, or any such thing," but that is "holy and without blemish." It is to see Himself perfectly reflected in all His saints.

And *before* He comes thus, His people must be in that condition. Before He comes we must have been brought to that state of perfection in the complete image of Jesus. Eph. 4:7, 8, 11–13. And this state of perfection, this developing in each believer the complete image of Jesus—this is the finishing of the mystery of God, which is Christ in you the hope of glory. This consummation is accomplished in the cleansing of the sanctuary, which is the finishing of the mystery of God, which is the final finishing of transgression, the making of a complete end of sins, the making of reconciliation for iniquity, the bringing in of everlasting righteousness, the sealing up of the vision and prophecy, and the anointing of the most Holy.

The present time being the time when the coming of Jesus and the restitution of all things is at the very doors; and this final perfecting of the saints having necessarily to precede the coming of the Lord and the restitution of all things; we know by every evidence, that *now* we are in the times of refreshing—the time of the latter rain. And as certainly as that is so, we are also in the time of the utter blotting out of all sins that have ever been against us. And the blotting out of sins is exactly this thing of the cleansing of the sanctuary; it is the finishing of all transgression in our lives; it is the making an end of all sins in our character; it is the bringing in of the very righteousness of God which is by faith of Jesus Christ, to abide alone everlastingly.

This blotting out of sins must precede the receiving of the refreshing of the latter rain. For it is only upon those who have the blessing of Abraham that the promise of the Spirit comes; and it is only those who are redeemed from sin, upon whom the blessing of Abraham comes. Gal. 3:13, 14. Therefore now as never before, we are to repent and be converted, that our sins may be blotted out, that an utter end shall be made of them forever in our lives, and everlasting righteousness brought in: and this, in order that the fulness of the outpouring of the Holy Spirit shall be ours in this time of the refreshing of the latter rain. And all this must be done in order that the harvest-ripening message of the gospel of the kingdom shall be preached in all the world with that power from on high by which the earth shall be lightened with its glory.

CHAPTER XVII

Conclusion

CHRIST the Lord, the Son of God, came down from heaven and was made flesh, and dwelt among men as the Son of man. This is an eternal fixture in the Christian faith.

He died on the cross of Calvary for our offenses. This is an eternal fixture of the Christian faith.

He arose from the dead for our justification. This is an eternal fixture in the Christian faith.

He ascended to heaven as our Advocate, and as such sitteth on the right hand of the throne of God. This is an eternal fixture in the Christian faith.

He is a priest upon His Father's throne—a priest forever after the order of Melchisedec. This is an eternal fixture in the Christian faith.

At the right hand of God, upon the throne of God, as priest upon His throne, Christ is a "minister of the sanctuary, and of the true tabernacle, which the Lord pitched, and not man." This is an eternal fixture in the Christian faith.

And He will come again in the clouds of heaven, with power and great glory, to take His people unto Himself, to present to Himself His glorious church, and to judge the world. This is an eternal fixture in the Christian faith.

That Christ lived in the flesh, died on the cross, rose from the dead, ascended to heaven, and sits on the right hand of the throne of God in heaven, must be an eternal fixture in the faith of every Christian, in order for that faith to be true and full.

That this same Jesus is a priest at the right hand of God on that throne, must be an eternal fixture in the faith of every Christian, in order for that faith to be true and full.

That Christ the Son of God, as priest at the right hand of God upon His throne, is there a "minister of the sanctuary, and of the true tabernacle, which the Lord pitched, and not man," must be an eternal fixture in the faith of every Christian, in order for that faith to be true and full.

And this true faith in Christ the Son of God *as that true priest,* in that true ministry, of that true sanctuary, at the right hand of the throne of the Majesty in the heavens; that His priesthood and ministry finishes transgression, and makes an end of sins, and makes reconciliation for iniquity, and brings in everlasting righteousness—this true faith will make *every comer thereunto perfect.* It will prepare him for the seal of God, and for the final anointing of the Most Holy.

By this true faith, every soul who is *of* this true faith can certainly know that in him and in his life, transgression is finished and an end of sins made; that reconciliation is made for all the iniquity of his life; and that everlasting righteousness is brought in to reign in his life for evermore. This he can know with perfect certainty, for the Word of God says so, and true faith cometh by hearing the Word of God.

All who are of this true faith can know all this just as truly as they can know that Christ is at the right hand of the throne of God. They can know it just as truly as they can know that He is Priest upon that throne. They can know it just as truly as they can know that He is there a "minister of the sanctuary, and of the true tabernacle, which the Lord pitched, and not man." And all this can be known just as truly as any statement of the Word of God can be known; for the Word of God plainly states it all.

Therefore in this time, let every believer in Jesus rise up in the strength of this true faith, implicitly trusting the merit of our great High Priest in His holy ministry and intercession for us.

In the confidence of this true faith, let every believer in Jesus take a long breath of restfulness forever, in thankfulness to God that this thing is accomplished: that transgression is finished in your life, that you are done with the wicked thing forever: that an end of sins is made in your life, and that you are free from it forever: that reconciliation for iniquity is made, and that you are cleansed from it forever by the precious blood of sprinkling: and that everlasting righteousness is brought into your life to reign for evermore, to uphold you, to guide you, to save you, in the fulness of that eternal redemption which, through the blood of

Christ, is brought to every believer in Jesus our great High Priest and true Intercessor.

And then in the righteousness, the peace, and the power of this true faith, let every soul who knows it spread abroad to all people and to the end of the world the glorious news of the priesthood of Christ, of the cleansing of the sanctuary, of the finishing of the mystery of God, of the times of refreshing come, and of the soon coming of the Lord "to be glorified in His saints, and to be admired in all them that believe . . . in that day," and to "present to Himself a glorious church, not having spot, or wrinkle, or any such thing," but "holy and without blemish."

"Now of the things which we have spoken this is the sum: We have such an High Priest, who is set on the right hand of the throne of the Majesty in the heavens; a Minister of the sanctuary, and of the true tabernacle, which the Lord pitched, and not man."

"HAVING THEREFORE, BRETHREN, BOLDNESS TO ENTER INTO THE HOLIEST BY THE BLOOD OF JESUS, BY A NEW AND LIVING WAY, WHICH HE HATH CONSECRATED FOR US, THROUGH THE VEIL, THAT IS TO SAY, HIS FLESH; AND HAVING AN HIGH PRIEST OVER THE HOUSE OF GOD; LET US DRAW NEAR WITH A TRUE HEART IN FULL ASSURANCE OF FAITH, HAVING OUR HEARTS SPRINKLED FROM AN EVIL CONSCIENCE, AND OUR BODIES WASHED WITH PURE WATER." AND "LET US HOLD FAST THE PROFESSION OF OUR FAITH WITHOUT WAIVERING; FOR HE IS FAITHFUL THAT PROMISED."

THE END.

More Choice Reading

THE GREAT CONTROVERSY
by Ellen White

The world is on the verge of a stupendous crisis. Here is the authorative answer to the confusion and despair of this tense age. Revealing God's ultimate plan for mankind, *The Great Controversy* may be the most important book you will ever read.

640 pages **$6.95**

THE DESIRE OF AGES
by Ellen White

This book is about the Man who stands at the center of all human history. No one else has had such a profound influence on the people of this planet as Jesus Christ.

768 pages **$6.59**

STEPS TO CHRIST
by Ellen White

Find a happy, fulfilling life by having a closer walk with Jesus Christ. An all-time best seller and classic.

$1.00 each

**Special price for bulk orders —
case of 100*   **$30.00 a case**

● *Available from The Upward Way or your local Christian bookstore.*

ELLEN, TRIAL AND TRIUMPH ON THE AMERICAN FRONTIER

by Paul B. Ricchiuti

Paul B. Ricchiuti

A unique look at Ellen White, a leading Christian writer. Colorfully written, *ELLEN* is filled with the atmosphere of the late 1800's. The book was written to show a little more of what Ellen White was like—not as a superwoman or stone saint, but as a real flesh-and-blood human being. Paul Ricchiuti is also the author of 16 children's books.

159 pages **$7.95**

NEW START!
NEW HEALTH, NEW ENERGY, NEW JOY!
by Vernon W. Foster, M.D.

The NEWSTART Lifestyle Program for renewed health, restored energy, new pleasure in living! You can begin to enjoy new vitality and freedom from illness with this valuable guide by Dr. Foster, currently with the renowned Weimar Institute in the foothills of California's Sierra Nevada Mountains.

269 pages **$9.95**

WHY JESUS WAITS
by Herbert E. Douglass

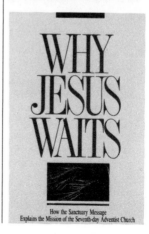

The message of the Sanctuary service has been largely missed or misunderstood by the Christian Church. Uplifting Jesus as the heart of the Sanctuary service, this book shows that from him comes an empowerment that enables the Christian to live a life like His. Moreover, it convincingly demostrates, in the light of the sanctuary service, that God is waiting for a people who will show that such lives can be lived.

92 pages **$3.95**